A NEW KIND
OF MAN

BOOKS BY JOHN CHARLES COOPER
Published by The Westminster Press

A New Kind of Man
Religion in the Age of Aquarius
The Turn Right
The New Mentality
Radical Christianity and Its Sources
The Roots of the Radical Theology

A NEW KIND OF MAN

BY
JOHN CHARLES COOPER

THE WESTMINSTER PRESS
PHILADELPHIA

Copyright © MCMLXXII The Westminster Press

All rights reserved—no part of this book may be reproduced in any form without permission in writing from the publisher, except by a reviewer who wishes to quote brief passages in connection with a review in magazine or newspaper.

Scripture quotations from the Revised Standard Version of the Bible are copyright, 1946 and 1952, by the Division of Christian Education of the National Council of Churches, and are used by permission.

ISBN 0-664-24943-4

Library of Congress Catalog Card No. 73-172906

BOOK DESIGN BY
DOROTHY ALDEN SMITH

Published by The Westminster Press ®
Philadelphia, Pennsylvania

PRINTED IN THE UNITED STATES OF AMERICA

This book is dedicated to the "goodly fellowship" of the prophets: M. L. King, the Berrigans, Malcolm X, Mead, Laing, Marcuse, Slater, Camus, Ferlinghetti, Goodman, Keniston, Newfield, and the Kennedys—some of whom already are enrolled in the noble army of martyrs.

> So God created man in his own image, in the image of God he created him; male and female he created them.—*Genesis 1:27*.

CONTENTS

Preface   11

1. The Shattering of the
   Traditional Images of Man   15

2. Transitions
   to the New Man   38

3. New Life-Styles
   for the Seventies   54

4. Life-Styles—
   The Informed and Conformed   89

5. Religion
   in an Aquarian Mode   126

6. The Present Revolution—
   A Dangerous Opportunity   145

Notes   163

PREFACE

This is a book with a philosophical viewpoint, a viewpoint much influenced by existentialism, written with a concern for other men. It sees man as the bearer of meaning in the world and indeed as the meaning of being. It sees man's inner world not as the pale reflection of an external material world that determines all things, but rather as the locus of freedom that interacts with the necessity of the material, external dimension.

The clearest influence on the thought presented here is the systematic theology and existential philosophy of Paul Tillich. With Tillich I see man as the multi-dimensional unity of all being. In man there is the complex organization of all the structures and organizations that make up the material and psychological world of the beings that lie around him in the universe. Just as Aristotle saw the human soul as made up of vegetable, animal, and rational elements, even so Tillich sees man as containing within himself all the elements that make up the inorganic, organic, and psychological worlds in a higher complex of organization that he calls spirit.

According to Jack Newfield, in his 1966 book, *A*

Prophetic Minority, the new radicals observe, with Lewis Mumford, that "modern Man has already depersonalized 'himself so effectively that he is no longer man enough to stand up to his machines.' "[1] Instead of this squelched, alienated, unhappy creature created by modern technology and the so-called scientific "objectivity" that has produced the Technocracy, Newfield, like his radically oriented peers, hopes for a new concept of man in which the importance of the individual is paramount, out of which the individual is able to achieve a society ("participatory democracy") where he can make the decisions that genuinely affect his life.[2]

And what of the great majority of the youth and younger people of our society (the *majority* under thirty) who are neither *New* Left nor *New* Right? Do they—the legions of consumers and enjoyers—have they any new ideas about man? I think so. I think the popularity of Marshall McLuhan's writings among the young is due to his diagnosis that Western civilization —up until recently—has produced a distorted type of human being who is all eye-oriented and cut off from the body's other senses. I think the significance of the success of rock groups like the Doors with their "The Soft Parade" and the music of Simon and Garfunkel lies precisely in the new conceptions of man that such musicians put forth. The popular music to which youth respond today is a popular music with genuinely poetic, even philosophical, lyrics. These songs cry out that all too many men and women in the twentieth century have depersonalized themselves, have—in Feuerbach's and Buber's terms—adopted an "I-It" style of life that slides quickly into an "It-It" relationship with the people of the world, cut off from one another by a mistaken "objectivity," and cut off from their own bodies by a culturally induced starvation of the tactile sense. Man wonders who he is, for he does not even know himself physically in a full way. *"What is man?"* is the unspoken question of every person alive today. There may have been eras characterized by the question of God; others may have been exercised by Pilate's question, "What is truth?" but our era asks insistently the question of man. With the psalmist we ask today, "What is man that thou regardest him?"

But we do not conclude with the same writer, "Thou hast made him a little lower than the angels"; for it is precisely the glory and the power man has garnered for himself that throws the whole human project into ultimate question.

What man is may indeed be gleaned from what man does; but we will argue here that what man believes, and hopes, and loves tell us more than deeds do, of what man is, and more importantly, of what man will become.

J.C.C.

Eastern Kentucky University

Chapter 1

THE SHATTERING OF THE TRADITIONAL IMAGES OF MAN

Modern philosophy likes to see the world in the manner of the characters in *Alice in Wonderland*—as two-dimensional, flat, and as made up of things that bear no exterior relationship to each other. Breaking language apart, playing games with words, the modern philosopher looks upon the more ambitious project of examining an "image of man" or a "concept of God" as unsophisticated. Yet it is at these higher levels, with these organic structures of thought, that we find the content of human beliefs, of ideologies, and of religious doctrines. Indeed, how we see man is basic to our vision of the world and of our own lives in general. If it is not part of philosophy's province today to study the gross structures of thought that make up our mental world, then too bad for philosophy: its horizon is not wide enough to help us now as it has helped man in the past. It is good for little or nothing, then, since it has no room for Socrates and Plato on the one end, and no room for us on the other.

The idea of an "image of man" may, however, be more theological than philosophical or even anthropological. Briefly put, an image of man is a basic mental picture of how a man thinks of himself and of other men.

What I mean by an image or vision of man is what the late Paul Tillich meant by a "view of man" in his 1965 seminar on "The Christian View of Man," held at the University of Chicago. In this sense of a "view of man," the basic Christian vision was one that "saw" man as having a threefold nature. This nature included the estimate that man was created good by God, created in the image of God, and that man was a complex creature formed of body and spirit. In contrast to this basic (or ancient) Christian vision, some philosophers also recognize a classical view or Greek vision of man and a "modern, scientific" view of man. The philosopher Harold H. Titus describes the classical view as chiefly interpreting man as a rational being. Most clearly to be seen in the dialogues of Plato, the Greek vision saw rationality as the highest part of the soul of man. In Aristotle's works, also, reason is the highest faculty of the human soul.

Mind is the unifying and organizing principle and, as such, is distinguished from the body. Reason is the pride and glory of man. . . . The intelligent man is the virtuous man. To know the right is to do it. Vice is the result of ignorance.[1]

In the modern, often called the scientific, view of man, we meet an image that demonstrates the power of man's reason by virtue of its completeness of detail, but that downgrades man's uniqueness, regardless of his rationality. The scientific view varies from one scientific discipline to another but agrees on certain

SHATTERING OF TRADITIONAL IMAGES OF MAN 17

basic points. First, man is a part of nature, and is subject to physical and chemical laws just like any other organism. Again, man is seen to be one of the animals that live on the earth. He is related to all the other living things he encounters. He is related most closely to the higher primates. The recent best seller, *The Naked Ape*,[2] made this relationship strikingly clear. At the same time, however, the physical and mental characteristics that set man apart from the other animals are recognized by the various sciences from physiology to anthropology.

The traditional images of man have been shattered by modern developments. The classical concept of the rational man, the Christian conception of man as a creation made in God's image, even the Renaissance ideal of man as Odysseus, set out on a lifelong voyage of adventure, have all crumbled. We are not overly impressed by man's rationality today, nor are the majority of Western men impressed by the divinity in man (although the members of the counter culture are). The deep thirst for security on the part of most men in the West seems to have killed the quest for adventure. But what conceptions about man have been put in their place? How do men see themselves in the last half of the twentieth century?

Basically, man sees himself in *historical, economic,* and *political* images, and these are almost exclusively materialistic symbols. We see ourselves as biologically determined, as economically formed and restricted, as politically motivated. The majority of men do not see themselves as spiritual beings. The declaration that "God is dead" followed quite naturally upon the almost universal denial that man is made in God's image.

Ancient man understood himself through the creation and recounting of myths. Most mythological stories about man's nature stress the paradoxical, if not positively contradictory, aspects of the human being.

The creation of man according to the Genesis myth came about when God the Creator breathed his Spirit into a physical frame made out of the dust of the earth. Man is, therefore, a creature akin to the beasts of the earth (and the earth itself) on the one hand, and akin to the Divine on the other.

According to the Babylonian myth of Adapa, man is the paradoxical combination of heavenly and earthly elements because of the lack of trust shown by Adapa, the first man. Adapa was sent to get from one of the gods a potion that would make him immortal. When Adapa, after great difficulty, got the potion, he feared to drink it, thinking it might be poison. By not drinking the potion, Adapa condemned himself to death.

Augustine's *Confessions,* with its autobiographical data and speculations on the nature of man, advanced the ancient insight that contradictory elements had free rein in man's being. Throughout the Dark Ages and the Middle Ages the ancient image of man remained unchallenged. The moral ambiguity of humankind was a root conception in Judaism, Islam, and in every form of Christianity, orthodox and heretical. Even Pelagianism, which claimed that man was fundamentally good, did not dispute the ambiguous nature of man's historical goodness. The sharp conflict between the more or less equal spiritual forces of good and evil seen by Manichaeism did nothing to remove ambiguity from man's nature.

The coming of the age of chivalry and the rise of

SHATTERING OF TRADITIONAL IMAGES OF MAN

national literatures in England, Spain, France, Italy, and Germany did little to change the West's outlook on man. Though basically good, man is still morally ambiguous. Sir Launcelot is brave, but his loyalty and truth don't quite cover his sexual temptations. Faust wants to know and to have power, but he is morally weak enough to sell out to the devil to attain these desires.

The Renaissance glorified man, to be sure, but did nothing to remove the ambiguity from man's nature, perhaps because that streak of ambiguity is the actual condition of man. In any event, the men who set out to conquer the world were very sure of what their intelligence and courage could accomplish, but never forgot they were mortal and fallible. Man was seen by the rising scientists and explorers as the receptor and effector of his world, but—as in Aristotle's philosophy—the world was seen clearly as outlasting man.

When the *Aufklärung* came on the Continent and the Enlightenment to the British Isles, a healthy cynicism about man's basic nature grew up alongside the belief in man's reasoning ability. No one has seen the paradox of human nature more clearly than Alexander Pope:

> Know then thyself, presume not God to scan;
> The proper study of Mankind is Man.
> Plac'd on this isthmus of a middle state,
> A being darkly wise, and rudely great:
> With too much knowledge for the Sceptic side,
> With too much weakness for the Stoic's pride,
> He hangs between; in doubt to act, or rest,
> In doubt to deem himself a God, or Beast;
> In doubt his Mind or Body to prefer,

> Born but to die, and reas'ning but to err;
> . . . .
> Created half to rise, and half to fall;
> Great lord of all things, yet a prey to all;
> Sole judge of Truth, in endless Error hurl'd:
> The glory, jest, and riddle of the world! [3]

The ages of Goethe, Hegel, Fichte, and Schelling also glorified man, and with the growth of Romanticism and the philosophy of Nature, began to lose the sense of man's moral ambiguity. Hegel forgot what Kant remembered: radical evil. Hegel forgot what Augustine never could forget: human sinfulness. Hegel's concept of the World-Spirit dissolved the connection of man to the earth and overstressed his connection to the Divine.

However, the nineteenth-century thinkers who were to have the most impact on the twentieth century were those like Nietzsche, Kierkegaard, Marx, and Engels, who dissolved the connection of man with the Divine and stressed the rootedness of man in the earthiness of history. (Kierkegaard, the Christian, was just as adamant in stressing the situation of man in history and his non-relationship to the Divine, as were the "atheists," Nietzsche and Marx.) Nietzsche and Marx made a radical break with all the dominant (respectable and prevailing) social traditions of Western culture. Nietzsche and Marx, therefore, sought the same goal as the earlier nineteenth-century Christian questioner, Kierkegaard. The philosophical quest of each of these thinkers—and of Engels after Marx—was not for a new system of ideas, or to create a new critique of human reason. Rather, each sought to create a new image of Man.

Henceforth, the Western philosophical quest becomes

SHATTERING OF TRADITIONAL IMAGES OF MAN

the same program as that laid down by the great religions: the creation of a new man. Before the coming of Kierkegaard, Nietzsche, Marx, and Engels, the aim of philosophy was to understand man and his world. With them—and afterward up to this day—the aim of the worldly-oriented philosopher is to change man and his world. No compromise between these two approaches was possible for them, and there still seems to be no viable third way. To the Christian, the dialectical materialist, and the proclaimer of a positivistic new morality, any cultural synthesis made up of Christian morality, the power of the new sciences, and liberal political views was neither possible nor desirable. None of these nineteenth-century thinkers were interested in being "helpful" or "understood." *They preached salvation for the human race by way of a complete change of mankind into a new kind of man.* They cared less about being successful than a Buddhist monk—they wanted their vision of a new man to succeed historically.

All of them—and Engels, Lenin, Unamuno, and the existentialists after them in the twentieth century—made valiant efforts to present clearly the human predicament: the state of spiritual and social alienation man had fallen into in the industrialized world. Kierkegaard best limned the spiritual dimension of this tragic self-estrangement. Nietzsche made the best case for the culpability of orthodox Christianity in inculcating a slave morality and a slavish mentality in man that split man's mind from its physical incarnation—the body. But of them all, Marx best diagnosed the illness of man in the Western social order, following Feuerbach (from whom we have received the category of I-Thou) and Hegel (who first laid out the phenomenon of alienation in his *Philosophy of Mind*). These did more than any other thinkers (with the exception of Freud) to prepare the way for new images of man in the twentieth century. Marx's dialectical materialism, with its "keys" to the understanding of all history, was a serious social-scientific effort to provide a verifiable theory of social change. But along with this positivistic center, Marx's thought is also inspiring and even charismatic. Marx's words cut to the quick even today because he was filled with the moral insight and the righteous outrage of Jeremiah, Amos, and Isaiah. He was, in short, a secular prophet.

In Marx, science, ethics, and the *telos*, or inner aim of human history, are presented as one grand design in which man participates willingly or unwillingly. Despite himself, the old man was becoming the new man, Marx declared, just as the sixteenth-century radical, Martin Luther, confessed: "The kingdom of God comes of itself without our prayers, but we pray that it might also come to us."

Today both ideologists and scientists, both theologians and atheistic philosophers are saying that *the direction and extent of human development is not predetermined by man's biological constitution*. Man's evolution is a matter of psychological development, not of physical development; it is spiritual and inward, not material—although the inner spirit is formed by the outer, material world. In the words of Kenneth Keniston, "the emergence of 'new' stages of life, can result from altered social, economic and historical conditions." [4] Keniston further observes that "human development can be obstructed by the absence of the necessary matrix, just as it can be stimulated by other kinds of environments." [5]

We are all familiar with the stunting of human development caused by the continuing existence of urban and rural slums, and the matrix of self-perpetuating poverty that is all too common—and unnecessary—in America. We are aware, too, of the red-hot overstimulation of human potential into precocious actuality in affluent suburbs, homes, and schools.

Perhaps the two most significant myths for the Western mind relating to human creativity and renewal in an imperfect cosmos are the stories of Prometheus and Christ. The story of the Christ is quite familiar (in broad outline) to almost every Western person, whereas the story of Prometheus may be known chiefly by the more highly educated. Christ represents the essence of creativity in human life: he was open, interested, courageous, loving, and forgiving. When his openness to others and his commitment to God and the future brings about his rejection and execution by the established powers, the Christ dies but is said to triumph over death by resurrection to a new mode of life. Renewal—indeed revolution itself—is thus seen in Christ's example of a dying to the ordinary life of the world and a rebirth to a new form of life. The struggle for the new, for an open future, is not defeated even by death in this basically optimistic and mystical vision of the ultimate meaning of human life.

The myth of Prometheus, on the other hand, is both historically older than the story of Christ and is more realistic in its reporting of the usual experience of human beings. Prometheus revolts against the established powers ("the way things are") and is caught and punished for his rebellion. Although said to be a demigod himself, Prometheus shows us the finest expressions of human nature in his generosity (he steals fire for man) and his courage (he never gives in). To punish his stubbornness, his suffering is made eternal. He is chained to a rock where a vulture continually devours his liver, which constantly regrows. Prometheus never experiences resurrection because he never experiences death. In this respect Prometheus is best seen as a symbol of the whole human race, which never dies but always suffers, while Christ is perhaps best seen as the symbol of the individual man.

However, both figures are "positive" (and for this reason very attractive) in that both are "good." Christ (also said to be "divine" as well as "human") is generous and forgiving. Prometheus is generous and helpful. Both figures are heroic in the deepest sense, since they both defy authority and violate the norm of their time and place for the sake of a greater good. Both suffer and bear it "manfully." And finally, both are said to be the beginning of new ages of world history. In both "heroes" the *new* breaks through and man advances toward freedom.

For some sixteen or seventeen centuries (from the fourth century A.D. to the early or middle twentieth century A.D.) the myth of the Christ dominated the mythic, artistic, and philosophic thought world of Western man, at first to a greater, then (since the sixteenth century) to a lesser degree. But this mythic domination never entirely suppressed the myth of Promethean man: the vision of man as religiously self-renewing, as rebel against God and cosmos in the name of man, the undefeated.

It is most interesting to note the need to reevaluate the Christ symbol as a heroic (even revolutionary) symbol in our time. Albert Cleage, Jr., the well-known exponent of a black theology, goes to great length to argue for a "black Jesus," precisely to establish the novelty and power for human progress included in the Christ symbol as well as to combat the "colorless" (and powerless) interpretation of the Christ figure by much of traditional Western Christianity.[6]

"Promethean man," in the sense that we are here using this name, is familiar to all of us. He is the black athlete giving the clenched-fist salute of the Black Power movement in the Mexico City Olympics. He is the peace marcher with the bloody head defiantly giving the "V-sign" of the peace movement. Promethean man is the "Yippie" student-age activist angrily giving the vulgar "finger" to the police during the 1968 Chicago convention troubles. Promethean men are the protesters, the resisters, the fighters for a new vision of what human society ought to be.

Perhaps the clearest and most attractive modern exemplar of Promethean man was Ernesto Che Guevara, whose death in a futile revolutionary attempt did nothing to diminish his attractiveness. In fact, there are many people in South America who do not believe, even now, that Che is dead.

In a fundamental psychological sense, the Promethean figure feels and accepts the fact that he must suffer, that he must accept what looks like historical defeat, but he is unable to conceive a genuine defeat, an ontological death. Similarly, those who are drawn to the Promethean symbol do not and cannot take death seriously, that is, as a bar to their apocalyptic expectations. The individual revolutionary may go down; a whole revolutionary generation may suffer defeat, but (as Marx insisted and now the Yippies insist) the revolution *must* ultimately succeed. To put our observations in a word, Prometheus, the rebel against heaven for the sake of man, is the mythological background for the twentieth-century image of revolutionary man.

The Physiology of Politics

If there is one revolution that has occurred in the past decade, it is the revolution in the way most North Americans look upon their bodies and feelings. This "new sensualism" is hardly brand-new, and yet its widespread acceptance and respectability are new. Often called "the *Playboy* Philosophy" when viewed from its sexual side, or "the Human Potential movement" when described from its psychological side, this new awareness of the physical stands in sharp contrast with the dualism of much older thought. The hedonism that many men and women have practiced in many times and places, but that never became the philosophical basis of any culture, has now been openly acknowledged as the foundation of the youth culture now building before our eyes. The natural enjoyment of young people of each other's company, companionship, and mutual sensuality is understandable, of course. But this is the first generation in which hedonism has become the basis of political ideology and religious doctrine—which is precisely what has happened. This is represented by the youth slogan (somewhat disguised here) that declares, "Sexual intercourse sets you free." There is, in short, a physiology of politics and we are experiencing today the effect of "sexual politics." [7] This urge toward sensual experience, expansion, and enjoyment, along with the sense of moral outrage [8] that constitutes the radical political impulse, gives power to the growing political unity of the counter culture.

Radical politics has a long history in the United States, despite the refusal of many leaders to admit it. The very revolution that brought the country into being was the result of radical political ideas—many imported from France—that swept over the colonies. Throughout the nineteenth century radical ideas gathered large followings, culminating in the alienation of section from section that ended in the Civil War. The rise of the labor movement, the struggle against child labor, the fight for the right to strike, the extension of the franchise to women, the imposition of the graduated income tax, and the legislation against monopolies, all eventuated from the spread and popularization of originally "radical" ideas. In a real way, even the conservatives of today are the children of yesterday's radicals.[9]

The development of a consistent radical tradition in America was retarded for almost two centuries because it was responsive to issues, and arose only when an issue was in the public eye (e.g., independence, slavery, the franchise for women), and subsided when the issue was pragmatically resolved. A genuinely radical party could come only when a philosophic base had been laid for it—a base that would not erode once the issue of the movement had been settled. The hedonistic search for experience of the whole person, body, mind, and spirit, social as well as personal, now has provided that philosophical base. Today, "reason," the shibboleth of both the conservative and the liberal, is considered suspect by both the young and the "intellectual" class in general.

Feelings, real human feelings, immediate feelings, are the sources that the bearers of the new mentality trust.

Western Christianity, in both its Catholic and its Protestant forms, has been largely committed to a dualistic view of human life from the very beginnings of its theological development until the mid-twentieth century. The shift away from dualism by many theologians, moralists, and church leaders in the past few decades represents one of the great traumatic changes in the intellectual basis of Western life. Briefly put, traditional dualism rests upon the heritage of ancient Greece, particularly upon Plato, rather than upon the Semitic background of Christianity. Platonic dualism evolves out of the basic belief that the mental and spiritual dimension is separate and separable from the physical, material dimension of man.

Plato, following the strong suggestions of Socrates as recorded in the *Phaedo,* holds that the soul (the mental and spiritual dimension) has a different origin from the body of man. The soul comes from the spiritual realm, "falling" into the body, as a prisoner into a prison, and must spend its earthly life striving to remain unsoiled by its contact with the physical. This soul is immortal, having both a preexistence (in "heaven") and a postexistence, surviving death. From this dualistic viewpoint, then, anything that smacks of the body or the material order is a lower degree of being and is antispiritual. On this basis, it is easy to see how the body and bodily processes, including sex, come to be seen as "sinful" and "shameful." Early Christianity, with its disdain of the pomp and pleasure of "the world" and its stress on the imminent apocalyptic end of the world, was naturally attracted to Platonic dualism. In fact, a Hebrew counterpart to Plato's dualism developed among the Essenes before the time of Christ, and an adaptation of Plato's doctrines to Judaism was made by the Jewish-Egyptian philosopher Philo in Alexandria during the first century A.D.

It should not surprise us that in its redefinition of man, the twentieth century is influenced by the pioneering work of the nineteenth century in psychology, and by the late nineteenth-century understanding of society and economics. Man, no matter who is doing the interpreting, can hardly be understood by the twentieth-century person except as a sexual being. Freud is determinative of at least part of man today in every man and not just in the Human Potential movement. It has become clear that human beings are not essentially disembodied minds but are total unities that have their basic levels in a physical realm. The emphasis upon getting in touch with our bodies in the Esalen movement is but a heightening of the knowledge that even neo-Thomist philosophers share.

If the emphasis upon man as sexual being were limited to the belief in, and the striving for, enjoyment and pleasure, then we might consider that emphasis to be overdone. But there is a much more profound element in the emphasis upon the body today, an emphasis that stems from Hegel and is developed in Marx, as well as in twentieth-century psychology. This emphasis is the theme of alienation.

The philosopher Hegel, though often despised by twentieth-century thinkers, is nevertheless given the honor of being followed in practice even when the follower does not realize his indebtedness. Hegel held that in the development of mankind there is a stage at which consciousness reaches the level of spirit and this spirit passes through a stage of self-estrangement.

In *The Phenomenology of Mind*, Hegel says that at the stage where the mind recognizes that the world is made up of a plurality of individuals, there is a sense of separation of self from self, of person from person, and of the self from its own foundation.[10] The very definition of a person, according to Hegel, is that he is a merely negative relation, a relation of exclusion from other persons. To be someone means not to be considered a part of a whole. To have self-identity is to consider oneself, and to be considered, as alien to other selves. The whole basis of legal systems and of justice and property rests on the statement that there is an absolute separation between one being and another, and that human beings have the power to split up and dispose of the real property in the world so that some is mine and some is yours and the greater part of it belongs to the others and not to me or to you.

Now this is a mental and intellectual state of alienation. Below this developed level of thought, indigenous to logic itself, is the concept, or the presupposition of all concepts, that there are: the self, and the object of thought; which makes their unity impossible. This is the whole basis of the idea that makes thought possible. This is the basis of distinctions made in thought, and it is difficult to see how there could be any thinking without it. Nevertheless, the subject-object dichotomy, as it is called, shows us that the very quest to know produces alienation.

SHATTERING OF TRADITIONAL IMAGES OF MAN

In a far deeper sense than Marshall McLuhan has it in his writings, thinking itself, and not just the presentation of information in written form, alienates man from the world and alienates man from man. Human reason, often worshiped as a good in itself, is not an unmixed good. For this reason Paul Tillich holds in his *Systematic Theology* that reason must find its depths in the dimension of spirit, in the event of revelation.

Of course, in the psychologists and psychiatrists, the original epistemological principle of Hegel is developed into a mental principle. Alienation becomes alienation of one part of man's mental equipment from another part of the same mind. Developed under the pressure of treating emotional illness, of which a high number of cases involve sexual inadequacies, psychologists extend the principle of alienation to cover the feeling of separation of mind from body, of person from physical function. In a similar way the economists and political scientists, following Marx, developed alienation as a sociological principle, especially in the realm of labor economics. For our purposes, we have no desire to deny the basic usefulness of alienation as a sociological category. Marx's analysis is highly creative and helpful and social scientists are not wrong in taking clues from it. On the other hand, Marxism in the pure sense of a philosophy, despite its widespread power in the modern world, is not as formative of modern images of man as one might think. It is, rather, the psychological use of the theme of alienation that is very determinative of modern concepts of man.[11] Since Marxist traditionalism tried to deny the validity of Western psychology for many decades, Marxism has been only immaturely developed. It is the psychoanalytic ideas that are influencing us today, and seemingly are now getting a hearing in Marxist countries also.

Alienation might be seen, in existential philosophical terms, *as modern man's basic way of being in the world.* Our very approach to nature and ourselves is a technological, manipulative, estranged one. As we approach social problems and the conquest of and the development of the environment, we do so in an alienated way. Our social institutions, by and large, are set up to reduce the interpersonal interaction of human beings for the purposes of efficiency and for the reduction of social friction. Even our attempts to overcome nonsensical historical patterns of segregation approached the problem in a technological and alienating way. We desire to mingle everyone together in order to reduce the chances of social friction and in doing so, to reduce the possibility of human interaction as well. This is by no means to say that we should not integrate our society: we should and must. It is simply to agree with the advocates of Black Power who say that to turn members of minority groups into more homogenized middle-class men, alienated from themselves and other people, is no big improvement for anyone.

The Connection of the Sexual Revolution and the Political Revolution

We have been treated to the declaration that we are living through a sexual revolution in our country, and to some degree this is probably true. However, it is probably also true that, in recent years, rather than there being a revolution in the manner of sexual relationships, there has been a revolution in frankness and in the willingness to write and talk openly about what has actually been going on for many years. But whatever finally is determined to be the case by such investigators as those at the Kinsey Institute, by Masters and Johnson, or by authors such as David Reuben, it is no doubt true that the hidden and repressed portions of human experience (at least as they were traditionally considered to be matters of privacy) are now exposed and open and no longer the occasion for shame. Recent films, plays, novels, songs, and even television programs leave little that can be improved upon in the way of frankness and openness.

Every city has a multitude of cinema houses offering the public what can only be described as pornographic movies. Better-made films such as *Catch-22*, *M*A*S*H*, *I Am Curious (Yellow)*, and others are just as explicit in their sexual material, even if they are not as crude as the so-called "skin flicks." But all this being the case, there is no noticeable decrease in human alienation. *Rather, the audiences who go to the skin flicks seem to me to be more alienated than the average run of the population.*

The popularity of the better-made movies of sexual content in no way guarantees that an act of Aristotelian catharsis is taking place in the audience. In fact, there is something inhuman (which may be the real meaning of pornographic) in the idea of middle-class, fully clothed, law-abiding citizens sitting side by side (and yet separated from each other even in a darkened, crowded movie house) watching what amounts to sexual fantasies being acted out by shadows flickering on a screen. It may well be that, rather than a sign of the overcoming of alienation, our current permissiveness is the mark of the acme of alienation.

The so-called sexual revolution has a political element precisely because it is a social phenomenon that expresses itself in attitudes and preferences, which can take political as well as economic forms. Indeed, the sexual revolution has a generation gap in it, although that generation gap is not so much one of age as of mentality. The old mentality in the sexual revolution expresses itself in watching films, reading *Playboy*, the sexually explicit novels, and the how-to-do-it sex books that are popular today.[12] It makes no difference whether these things are seen or read to be enjoyed, or to be condemned. It really makes no difference if they are not seen at all but only heard about and criticized. The method of responding to them is the key.

On the other hand the bearers of the new mentality enjoy sex films and find them funny because of the contrast between what they portray and what is actually the case in the lives of many people in our culture. Seeing these sexually permissive things makes little difference to such people, because already in their lives they engage in whatever kind of activities they desire. There's no need for them to find relief in a movie or book.

Life-Styles, Not Cultures

Philip Slater, in his excellent analysis of American culture at the breaking point, *The Pursuit of Loneliness*,[13] observes that this generation has experienced a change in values. He says:

SHATTERING OF TRADITIONAL IMAGES OF MAN 35

The major change seems to me to be a strengthening of the feeling side of the human-need-versus-social-form conflict. For the older generation rituals, ceremonies, and social institutions have an intrinsic validity which makes them intimidating—a validity which takes priority over human events. . . . The younger generation experiences a greater degree of freedom from this allegiance. . . . Their attitude is more secular—social formality is deferred to only when human concerns are not pressing.[14]

C. P. Snow became famous (in the 1950's) for observing that the twentieth century has two cultures, a humanistic one that attempts to continue the artistic and literary (and to some extent, the religious) traditions of the past, and a scientific culture that is (supposedly) present- and future-oriented and concerned only with manipulation of the environment.[15] Snow implied pretty clearly that all is up for us if we don't get the two cultures into cooperative communication with each other. So fast does history leave its prophets behind that the "two cultures" of C. P. Snow exist now (if they have ever really existed outside the shallow snobbery that is the occupational disease of professors in colleges of arts and sciences) only among the generation over forty. For the members of the now generation *there is no such separation of the humanities and sciences.* It was on the basis of a unitary view of culture that the giant Earth Day program was instituted in April, 1970.

This united vision of life lies behind the frank acceptance of the new honesty in sexual matters on the part of the bearers of the life-style I call the "new mentality." Since the spiritual and the physical are seen as one, there is no need to suppress one dimension and enhance the other. Thought has physical expression; so does prayer. Worship has all the elements of life in it, which is communicated in a heavy, rather gross way by the parody of the Holy Communion and resurrection that forms a major part of the current "hip" movies. "All is one" is not just a useless comment from a fogged mind; it is the major philosophic principle of the new mentality.

Beyond the Split of Prometheus and Christ

We began this chapter with reference to the cultural myths of Prometheus and Christ. These basic myths of the nature of man have usually been kept separate in Western thought. Occasionally, elements of the two myths have been brought together, as in *Don Quixote*. In Cervantes' novel, the humorous, pathetic elements of the Christ and the absurdity and frustration of Prometheus are unified. Today, Christ and Prometheus are closely identified indeed, but with less of the pathetic and more of the tragic—as well as the optimistic elements—made prominent. William Hamilton and Paul van Buren, following Dietrich Bonhoeffer, make such a unification in the symbol of "the Man for others."

The unity of the characteristics of Prometheus and Christ in a character like Don Quixote can be seen in literature, but it can also be seen in the flesh in the life-style of many "hip" younger (and older) people. The pointlessness of wildly idealistic visions and quests and the cultivated quietness and harmlessness of one who knows he has found the secret of life can be seen

SHATTERING OF TRADITIONAL IMAGES OF MAN

among these young people. This is a new man with a new form of consciousness. This new consciousness has ushered in a new philosophy and a new life-style. We shall consider this philosophy and these life-styles in the next two chapters.

Chapter 2

TRANSITIONS TO THE NEW MAN

We have seen that the older, foundational conceptions of the nature of man have suffered erosion in the twentieth century. It is not too strong a characterization of the "lost" feelings of many contemporary people, especially youth, to say that their image of man has been shattered. The generation growing into manhood around us shows many of the characteristics of the returning combat veteran of every period: they are disillusioned with what they were taught as children, they are groping for some new symbols to fill the spiritual vacuum in their lives. Men and women, young and old are wrestling today, going through a transitional, searching phase, trying to discover a vision of humanity that has the power to sustain their lives.

One of these groping people has put the problem of the multitude of new symbols of meaning today in these words:

> People formulate so many theories
> Try to find what's real,
> but listen, hear me
> Theories still aren't facts

> Sometimes we treat
> them like they are.[1]

The crux of the problem of man's meaning or lack of meaning lies in the fact that *men* offer up symbols of that meaning to themselves and to other men. The experience of meaning or meaninglessness comes only when one accepts—or rejects—the symbols and images put into social use by other human beings, or "invents" some of his own. We might paraphrase Jean-Paul Sartre and say, "Man means whatever man wants himself to mean." This is obviously quite unsatisfactory, both in terms of consistency and social utility as well as in personal terms. Socrates pointed out this unsatisfactory situation when he criticized the Sophists who taught that "man is the measure of all things." If man is the only measurement, then it is difficult to decide how to measure man.

The later twentieth century has seen, therefore, a period of widespread experimentation with symbols and images of man, expressed mainly in the trying out of new life-styles. We will discuss some of these life-styles more thoroughly in the next two chapters. Here we wish to explore some of the social and ideological elements that have made these transitional experiments possible and necessary. First we should make some remarks upon the political environment in which conceptions of man arise.

Political Environments

Man has lived in many political environments, beginning with the kind of basic decisions that led him from the forest and steppes to a more settled life in the cave. Yet, political environments, up to the period of the French and American revolutions, were restricted, finite circles that embraced as members only the elites of the human community. The only persons who were fully "persons," in the Western, twentieth-century sense, were those who had achieved, by virtue of superior physical strength or accident of birth, some leverage of social power. As examples, we might consider the situation in Egypt, reported in the Old Testament. The political environment was restricted, including as members of its class the Pharaoh, his family and advisers, the priests and seers, and the military officers. Everyone else was a nonpolitical person, a subject, serf or slave. But it was possible, the book of Genesis tells us, for one of great intelligence and unusual gifts to be brought into the political class. This is what happened to Joseph (Gen., ch. 41). In another fashion, by the cunning of his mother, Moses also became a member of the class wielding political power (Ex., ch. 2). But Moses' condition was marginal and he lost his place in the "establishment" environment (Ex. 2:15). His intelligence and gifts were such, however, that he was able to build a counter environment of power, one that eventually succeeded in establishing a new religion and a new nation-state. The story of that development is the basis of the Old Testament.

At the beginnings of the Anglo-Saxon development of democratic principles, the political environment was fairly limited to the king and the higher ranks of nobility and clergy. The Magna Charta, forced on the king at Runnymede, actually expanded only slightly the class wielding political power, by bringing the barons and lesser nobility into the privileged circle. However, the principles forced upon the king by the have-not nobles proved to be the foundations for that explosion of political growth which has ultimately resulted in the well-nigh universal franchise in Anglo-Saxon nations.

After the rise of socialist and democratic ideas in comparatively modern times, the political environment underwent a growth explosion of geometric proportions. The Western concept of the "citizen" who had the franchise laid the foundations for that participatory democracy which has been the ideal and the seemingly impossible goal of social idealists throughout the eighteenth, nineteenth, and twentieth centuries.

The story of the growth of modern civilization, in human terms, is not restricted to developments of new tools, techniques, and territories, but is basically that of the expansion of political power among ever larger and larger groups within nation-states. The great rise of the middle class that eventually won the balance, then the bulk of political power from the nobility and clergy, *is* the history of Great Britain and France. It is the immediate background of the histories of the United States, Canada, Australia, and New Zealand. The tortured history of the struggle to overcome human slavery in the nineteenth century is, at bottom, part of this geometric progression of the growth of the political environment. In the twentieth century this growth has been among women, minority groups marked by color, the young, and the peoples of former colonial territories. We are still living through this period of rapid political expansion. The stresses and strains of this growth give our time both its interest and color as well as its discomfort and dangers.

Political Change—The Life of the Social Organism

In another study,[2] I tried to impress upon our conscious understanding of our times the fact that the *conservative* political mentality exists for, and supremely desires, *change—social change*—just as much as the *liberal* or *radical* mind. Social change is to the group organism we call a state (or community) what the vital signs are to a single, living organism. For this reason, the concept of the status quo never refers to a stabilization of a social situation, but always to a change away from a present social situation with which the conservative is disturbed. To be "for" a status quo means, in psychological terms, that the type of "status" the conservative desires is already in jeopardy, and thus he wants to regress society's forms to a previous state, or to advance society to a new set of forms that better fit his ideals. Since time travel is asymmetrical—i.e., only possible in one mode, travel toward the future—this means that "reaction" or "regression" are meaningless terms. Actually, the conservative cannot move society back to the past even in its exterior modes, for men *do* have memories. Therefore, the conservative program is actually a plan to develop an alternative future through social changes beneficial to him and his group. At least he *believes* such changes to be beneficial, even if they are not.

To some degree, every year of human experience is marked by change. There have not been, at least within history proper (i.e., the span of recorded human thoughts and acts), any periods that experienced no change at all. Yet social change is a matter of varying rates. Some periods of history exhibit slow, and therefore only occasional, changes. Other periods show relatively more rapid social changes, which makes for a high frequency of new problems. The periodicity and ratio of social change are functions of the human consciousness and its investigation of the novel elements in its experience. The relative rate of social change is *not* a function of the development of new techniques and technologies as Marx, Lenin, and McLuhan tell us; rather, the development of such new techniques and technologies are the instruments of social change. They are consequently of a second order of importance when compared to the evolution of the human consciousness that devises these tools and techniques. Man creates new instruments and processes precisely to realize in the concrete dimension of existence what he has imagined in the dimension of mind. Before there was a light bulb there was the idea of one, and the belief that one could be brought into existence in the concrete dimension. Edison first imagined the light bulb, then set out to discover if it could be turned into concreteness or fact. He didn't "just discover" it. Nothing of man's cultural heritage is "just discovered." It is dreamed first; then, if it meets certain criteria of logic and physics, it can be "found."

Social change is thus a product of the mind of man first and foremost; not of technology, economic necessity, or of any other single or multiple material, deterministic force. It is the virtue of the New Left and the New Right, in America and abroad, that both groups understand this psychological fact. They have "kicked" the drug of materialism that forms the dogmas of the old left and the old right. Adolf Hitler and Joseph

Stalin were exceptions in the older order, for they recognized the primacy of the mental or spiritual in building new life-styles and thus of forming a new man. Unfortunately Hitler and Stalin were psychotic and demonic and used their knowledge to create concrete, historical evil.

Among the moral and constructive leaders of men, only the Kennedys exhibited this basic insight in their conduct of national affairs. Happily, this secret is "breaking through" into the consciousness of many younger politicians today. Eugene McCarthy surely knows the primacy of the spiritual over the material in human affairs but has so far shown himself unable to translate his insight into significant, successful action.

As a working definition, we may refer to any leader who recognizes that it is the mentality of man that must be changed *before* society can be changed, as a charismatic leader. It is *insight* and not some mysterious fascination of personality that makes the attractiveness (and dangerousness) of such a charismatic person a concrete, historical reality. The paradigmatic models of such insightful *moral* leaders in Western history are, of course, Socrates, Moses, and Jesus Christ. Eastern history also has its great examples: Buddha, Confucius and Lao-Tse.

The Primacy of the Spiritual Over the Material

One thread runs true throughout the many transitional, experimental visions of man that have been proposed and "lived through" in the past decade. This thread is the generation-wide belief in the primacy of the spiritual, inward elements of human life over the material ones. The lyrics of many rock songs, the poems of Rod McKuen, and the personal expressions of many young persons all show this turn toward the spiritual.

One college freshman expressed her search for the spiritual in life in the following words:

> Contemporary society has been compared to "clouds of mystery" and "confusion on the ground" where we all wonder, "Who'll Stop the Rain?" In this song, the writer says that for as long as he can remember there have been such clouds and confusion, and that men have been trying to find the sun down through all the ages. It's interesting how such symbols as the sun or light, and the rain are used to symbolize happiness and sadness. . . . "The windows of the world are filled with rain. . . ."
>
> On a much deeper level, the rain is indicative of the frustrations and pain of life; an example of a slow death. The sun, though, would represent the truth, or the light that leads us out of darkness. Obviously, this sun could be God.
>
> "When you feel like you've been mistreated, and when your friends turn their backs on you—let the Sun shine in." So say the lyrics of the famous record of the year 1969, "Aquarius." Songs like this offer part of the answer to our problems today. If the sun is to mean God, then we are all urged to allow God to come into our lives to help us achieve "harmony and understanding . . . and the mind's true liberation" [3]

This same young lady goes on to give a philosophical justification for her search for the "light," for the spiritual element in the world:

> From Plato we get the parable of the cave, where there is a material sun and an eternal Sun of truth.

All human beings are chained in a cave, which represents the universe. They can only look straight ahead, where they see images reflected on a wall from objects being passed in front of a huge fire located behind them. Since everyone is chained, no one knows the answers to life's questions anymore than anyone else. It would seem logical to ask a person who had managed to break away from the chains and climbed out of the cave to where the true light or Sun was. This Sun is truth; God. But the people in the cave do not like to be reminded that they live in darkness, in need of the light. . . . "And men loved the darkness rather than light, because their deeds were evil."

Light is the essence of the divine. The beam is one of great clarity and man, if he looks too closely, will be shown the truth of his life here and there. The blind are the uncaring, for they see not what is placed before them. They are the ones of hate, and love. They are infinitely endeavoring to close themselves from the truth and the good and to shut their hearts to the aching of the world surrounding them. I fear for their souls. They can be lost today for they may never have a tomorrow.

The Sun people or prophets were ridiculed and laughed at and eventually killed because they told the people what they didn't want to know.[4]

This young person *has already identified herself* with a counter-cultural movement that is devoted to the exploration of the spiritual dimension of man. She and thousands like her look at their parents, teachers, and other adults around them and see only spiritual barrenness. They turn for their guidance to those who sing and write of the feelings of the heart, the sensitivity of the mind and the freshness of the physical senses. Such young people and their older allies identify with the critics of our society, for they believe:

> The Sun people have the only opinion which counts, since the Sun houses the truth and the spiritual standards of life. Such Sun people as Christ and Socrates came back not to condemn, but to save. "Send me to reflect your light in the darkness of futility, mere existence, and the horror of casual human cruelty. . . . Give me your light, Lord." When one is touched by the Sun, he is no longer selfish, but genuinely concerned about the welfare of others. Normal drives for success are no longer the main motivation. But since insecurity is one of our main problems, we are afraid of critics and those who really "tell it like it is." [5]

A Modern Conversion Experience

The following observations are made by a young male student from a Midwestern university. A high achiever, who has traveled abroad, he left the university for one semester, then returned. His report on his life-style reveals the pull of genuine, personal religion on many young people today. This young man tells us of a migration from faith to unfaith and a life-style which later disgusted him, and a "conversion" to his original faith again. His story is not unlike that recounted by Augustine in the *Confessions:*

> Being reared in the church I was familiar with the status quo morality of America and being a "Christian." For some reason I had a rebellious attitude, somewhat

suppressed, inside me, and I directed my activities and desires in exact opposition to that which I was taught. I began drinking heavily and fighting for no reason. I hurt many friends and my parents. At the same time I was hurting all these people by drinking, fighting and using vulgar language, I was in danger of prison for my sexual escapades. I felt as if the whole world was falling in on me. I needed a way out and I realized that another lie, bottle of beer or joint was not going to provide it. I believe I did reach the bottom. I was desperate. Nothing my parents could say was able to soften that heartache and ultimate loneliness which I was experiencing. Finally I turned to that which I had rejected all my life, I turned to God. I prayed with a friend and I put everything on the line. At that point I realized what I was doing. I was humbling myself. I never was able to do that before. This was no synthetic experience brought on by a "nothing better to do" attitude, rather it was a plea to God—and to my friends—for help.[6]

The experience of this young man is by no means unique. We see many such "conversions," from meaningless lives to faith, from belief in war to the embracing of pacifism, from a desire for material success to entry into the Peace Corps.

The student concludes by observing:

The change of heart I experienced has given me a new life-style which has totally changed my outlook on life. I call this life-style "Christianity," but I want to define what I mean by this. The characteristics of a Christian are humility, frugality, love and obedience. One may say that a lot of people live that way and are completely ignorant of any religious doctrines. The difference, which makes a Christian stand in contrast to that type of person, is his attitude. That involves rebirth, repentance, or as some people call it, "getting your head on straight." I believe that the ground rules to this type of life-style are found in the New Testament. The first is to love God more than anything. The second is to love your neighbor more than yourself. This is my life-style and I think it answers many of the questions that the now generation is asking.[7]

This young person has passed through a great transition, from hedonism to moral responsibility, from aimless wandering to an inward discipline.

Reading the record that these young people freely give of their own inner and outer struggles, I realize that they know as much of the terror and agony of the quest to be a man as Nietzsche, Sartre, Camus, and Marcel. Over the "generation gap" that separates us from these rightly troubled young people, we feel the genuineness of their search for a way to become fully human. Those of us who, though over thirty, share the "new mentality" of modern youth feel that it is now time for the church and American society to wake from sleep. Miguel de Unamuno once wrote that it is the first duty of the Christian to wake the sleeper, when that sleeper lies on the edge of an abyss. The abyss of dehumanization and the loss of every Christian and human value lies before us as a genuine possibility. The continuing war in Asia and the erosion of democratic practices and values at home should outrage us. We have not yet, as a people, genuinely considered what it means "to be a man."

Other Alternatives in Experimental Living

It seems that the life-style which one has, is much determined by one's reaction to criticism. Another factor is the value placed on material things and economic needs. These factors influence what the person thinks about, and this in turn influences his life-style. The "straight people" seem to be conforming to a common goal, and this could be good. But it also seems that "straight people" have their beliefs fixed without thinking much about them. Those who resent this conformity and desire independence choose alternative life-styles.

Unfortunately, the alternative life-styles are frowned upon by the straight society. Some who have thought about the wrong things (such as ending a war) have been shot down in the interest of the silent majority. Incidents such as these lead to thoughts of radical hate or even revolution. Such thoughts cause some to have a life-style that is dominated by resentment of the present authority and dreams of their own authority.

The life-style of revolutionary thinking is common among many college "long hairs." Some "long hairs" are concerned students of politics who recognize the madness and emptiness of a society that tolerates immorality and blind cruelty. They resent the fact that each generation of young men is expected to fight an unknown enemy, simply because a whole country has been called "evil." They also see the inequality of men and the results of racism in America. The "revolutionaries" say they are "fed up." They would probably be in sympathy with, or join a violent organization. Until they get leadership, however, they protest by their dress and drug use.

While they do protest by being "freaks" and getting together to "drop acid," "smoke grass," or snort heroin, they have not freed themselves and they know it. They have to eat and find shelter. For this reason they must conform to some degree by working. Thus they contribute to capitalism by making money for their employers.

A Growing Independence Without Radicalism

There are many shades of transitional experience between the out-and-out rebel and the deeply religious, almost mystic, young person. Here is a statement from a young woman who is somewhere in the middle of the spectrum of life-styles. She has moved a long way from a childhood spent in religious fundamentalism.

I guess my friends would be considered straight as far as some of the new life styles are concerned. I don't think they would join a commune. All of them want a marriage and a family situation much like that of their parents, but they do differ from the older generation in the basis for their goals. Those around me seem to be very sensitive to what they believe to be right for them. More and more, I see kids who really have opposite opinions and philosophies enjoying these differences and accepting them as a part of each other. No one tries to impose his ideas on anyone as much as they like to discuss them. A person who is so impressionable as to adopt someone else's beliefs instead of establishing his own is rejected by nearly every type of person. I guess this comes under, "doing your own thing." It sounds really cliché, but no one admires or can even like a copycat. It doesn't matter so much what you think in relation to anyone else, but the fact that you do think for yourself—that is important. Maybe this is one reason why many are getting away from drugs. With the emphasis on individuality, a person who is honestly searching for his own life style must do it his own, individual way—not the way so many have tried which is drugs. The pure person is the most "real" being, not a person who has added drugs that may distort the "real" being that you are.[8]

Our moderate co-ed goes on to observe that young people who copy the styles of dress, speech, drug use, and the affectation of social alienation—when it is not truly their own conviction—are to be pitied. She sees the lockstep conformity of much youthful nonconformity and turns away from its "plasticness."

Causes have gotten into the same stereotype that clothes have. So many people protest and join movements simply for the identification and current popularity of the event. If people could be honest and concerned with what they think and believe instead of worrying over public opinion, perhaps we could realize a more satisfying existence. I think all of this goes into a life style which stresses personal honesty. I want to see and decide for myself, and try not to kid myself about the way things are just because they may not be too pretty. I suppose no really permanent decisions can ever be made with this philosophy because new things will always be coming up to change other factors. But if drastic change must come, I think I can accept it by believing in this way.[9]

Man is, and always will be, faced with the need to make choices. He must choose between the conflicting claims of many philosophies, political parties, and religions, as to who man is. He must choose the ideal or ideals to which he will commit his life. History seems to indicate that even when man makes such a choice of ideals seriously, in fear and trembling, in pride and hope, he never fully realizes them. Man never reaches his deepest, most precious goals, but he does become like his ideals and goals. Man's true end is always "out there" before him, an unreached, unreachable lure. Yet, in this project of choice, the man who falls short of his goal is not thereby made unhappy or ignoble. He is not to be pitied. Only the one who makes no effort, dreams no dreams, forces himself into no chosen project is to be pitied. Such a conformist, such a drifter, has missed the terror and the beatitude of a human being becoming a man.

In the next chapter we must explore more fully some of the nonconforming choices made by young people in our time. The new life-styles of the 1970's reveal the choice of ideals and goals that our disturbed and sensitive children have made. We need to understand these new life-styles and the people who create them.

Chapter 3

NEW LIFE-STYLES
FOR THE SEVENTIES

If we were to give a title to the historical period 1960–1972, it would probably be "The Period of Revolution and Counter Revolution." To say this, however, would mean using the terms "revolution" and "counter revolution" in senses different from those given them in Marxist (and military) terminology. All sectors of American society use the term "revolution," but there is little common content in the popular uses of the word. We need to get clear just what we mean when we speak of the "youth revolution" and the conservative "counter revolution" before we can genuinely understand the *political life-style of the 1970's.*

"Revolution" is a powerful word. It is not a dull, emotionless term. "Revolution," when used in some contexts, as in a discussion of the "American Revolution" (or "War for Independence"), is a "good" word with hallowed connotations. Proper, conservative ladies and gentlemen gladly claim to be "Daughters (or Sons) of the American Revolution." The term, to them, means the assertion of the dignity of their families and their personal beliefs and privileges over against the real or supposed oppression of the British Crown in the 1770's or of other threatening forces in our own day.

"Revolution" when used by the recently awakened political groups such as blacks, Mexican-Americans, Puerto Ricans, and radical youth organizations means something far different. For some of these groups, "revolution" may have exactly the meaning given the term by the dictionary:

> A sudden, radical, or complete change. . . . A fundamental change in political organization; *esp:* the overthrow or renunciation of one government or ruler and the substitution of another by the governed.[1]

The synonym of revolution, in this sense, is rebellion.

There have been, and now are, some few individual radicals (on both the extreme left and the extreme right) who have used "revolution" in this classic sense —and meant it. Some of the black radicals who have fled the country undoubtedly do mean "Let us rebel" when they cry "Revolution." But most users of the word do *not* mean rebellion in the classic sense. In this ambiguity lie some of our deepest social and political problems.

"Revolution," in the 1970's sense of the term, is for the majority of young people at once a *less* threatening and a more ominous word than the Marxist term. The "movement" or the "revolution" through which we have been passing for some time now is not a centrally directed, systematic attempt to overthrow the existing legal system and power establishment by traditional physical means. Rather, it is an attempt to establish a "counter culture" or "alternative life-style" alongside, beneath, above, and within the present power system.

Indeed, there is not just *one* counter culture or "alternative America" being proposed, but a whole series of different alternative life-styles that are being devised on a trial-and-error basis by small groups of alienated people all over the country.

Why are there such attempts to create new or alternative life-styles? Perhaps this quote from R. D. Laing, the British psychiatrist, about his own country is also true of the United States and Canada, and contains the answer:

> A child born today in the United Kingdom stands a ten times greater chance of being admitted to a mental hospital than to a University, and about one fifth of mental Hospital admissions are diagnosed schizophrenic. This can be taken as an indication that we are driving our children mad more effectively than we are genuinely educating them. Perhaps it is our way of educating them that is driving them mad.[2]

Especially among the youth confined to the vast social institutions called "universities" that arose (with that parallel institution, the prison), in modern times, there is now going on a search for an alternative style of life that will keep one from going mad. A national sample of college students in 1970 showed that 48 percent of those entering college that year planned to join a fraternity or sorority, whereas a previous sample a few years before showed that only 27 percent planned such an association. Why the change? Because the need for an intensely personal, small social group is keenly felt by college (and high school) youth today. Additionally, the college fraternity and sorority system extending from campus to campus provides a channel and a cover for traffic in marijuana and drugs. A little investigation reveals that the more "normal" appearing fraternity man is just as alienated as the "freak" or hippie nonjoiner.

"Revolution," in the usual youth sense, then, is really equivalent to cultural "subversion" or to an attempt to ignore completely the culture and power structure all around us, while creating new ideas, groups, and social forms that are more suited to meet personal and social human problems.

Hope vs. Hopelessness

The differences that exist between individual young people (and older people who also share in the new consciousness or the new mentality) are real and deep. The bearers of the new mentality do not form a homogeneous social group, but are split down the middle, socially and individually, into the active and passive approach to the corporate superstate we all inhabit. Again, within the two wings of the youth movement, there are profound differences of emphasis. Although foreign to most of the elements that make up the hippie mind-set, violence increasingly has appeared in hippie circles. Again, although all activistic bearers of the new mentality are for positive, overt action, very few have seriously contemplated violent action against the rest of our society, and fewer still have actually engaged in it. The paradoxes of passive/active, nonviolent/violent run throughout the American youth culture including the university and high school communities and the society of street people. The one set of parameters that can be applied to the movement is the tension between "hope" and "hopelessness" in the face of our society's problems.

Basically, the young person who seeks to create an alternative life-style, whether it is a politically oriented one or not, still shows hope for the future, although he may have little hope for present society. It is the hopeless who offer us no alternatives but violence. The discredited Weathermen (a faction of the old Students for a Democratic Society) represent the fullest extent of this sense of futility. The explosion of their underground bomb factory in New York City clearly expresses the end result of the appeal to violence in our current situation.

Joseph Sittler, a Lutheran theologian at the University of Chicago, has warned against the American weakness for flight from problems by "moving on," either west or to the suburbs. His words are equally applicable to the temptation to violence:

> Our entire American history has been lived out, until recently, within a huge land within whose seeming illimitability we could flee the tasks of justice and the works of love by flight into space. The frontier was always there; if time's problems in Detroit made life with the fellowman a burden, there was always the frontier, the west, or the suburb.
>
> "It is now time to wake out of sleep." Man in space can evade issues; man in time must deal with them where he is. Space offers options that may be realized by moving; time stands as a symbol for that accomplishment of community which must be done where one is. This is America's challenge translated out of the apostolic word—the time is at hand. Can the spirit that settled a continent settle the less romantic but

tougher and holier issues that alone can sustain a national community?[3]

Campus Unrest

It seems somewhat strange at this point in time to speak of campus unrest. For one who has spent the past dozen years in college teaching and watched the "quiet" generation of the late 1950's give way to the "active" generation of the late 1960's, this seems like a very "calm" time. I hesitate to say too much, lest the spell break and problems arise again. And yet the quiet of the fall, 1970, semester was broken on fifty-eight American campuses by various kinds of disturbances. The spring of 1971 also witnessed many protests after the mass arrests of peace marchers in Washington, D.C. The "quiet" we are told about by the mass media is, in short, only a relative quiet, compared to the past few troubled years.

If there has been a softening of campus dissent since the spring of 1970, it is probably due to philosophical rather than political factors. The basic thrust of students now seems to be toward the inward and the personal, rather than toward the active and confrontational as a life-style. This shift toward the inward is marked by the rise of interest in mysticism and speaking in tongues, toward "revivals" and "Jesus Freak" mass baptisms and street-corner witnessing (spreading from California to the East Coast), and, among the unconventionally religious, toward occult practices including witchcraft and astrology. This inwardness is both fostered by, and tends to foster, unfortunately, a continuing experimentation with marijuana and drugs on the part of a significant number of college students.

We cannot rule out altogether, however, a "heating up" of the campus scene at any time. It is possible that adverse developments in the Indochina war might raise significant issues among large campus groups. Indeed, an increase in fighting in Asia by U.S. troops might give the university as many headaches as it would give the Pentagon. No academic year, for years to come, will be free of some acts of protest against either domestic or international policies of the United States Government.

With the recent passing of the war issue from the front line of "campus causes," and even of a de-emphasis on the draft as a major issue, we must see the university itself, its teaching methods, its professors, and its government as the chief areas that may (and already have) come into campus contention by younger faculty and the student body.

Roots of Campus Unrest

Nathan Glazer, writing in the November, 1970, issue of *Tempo*,[4] identifies six roots of campus trouble. His analysis is so well done that we would like to discuss his six points here.

Glazer identifies the first root of campus unrest as *the crisis over the function of higher education*. We are living in a time of mass education, but we cannot assume any longer that everyone on campus wants to take a Ph.D. The fact is, many go to college and don't know why, and many colleges have been built and don't know why they exist. The country is full of institutions that were once good teachers colleges and are now, at ten times their former size, only pale imitations of universities.

The second root of campus unrest is *the issue of free speech and political activity on campus*. The 1964 problem at the University of California at Berkeley was over free speech and the right to collect funds for political purposes on campus. Actually these funds were desired to support civil rights work. This issue has been partly settled now, since peaceful demonstrations on campus are now accepted in most places. However, anyone who knows the campus scene would find it hard to believe that there is complete freedom of speech and assembly on many campuses. The memory of Kent State, Jackson State, Orangeburg, South Carolina, and other incidents of official violence might well be the reason for the relative "quiet" on campus since the summer of 1970.

The third root of trouble on campus is the *continuing problem of the blacks* and other minority groups in America. The old civil rights movement is largely gone now, but black students are freely organized into often militant black student unions everywhere. The demand for separate and special classes, dorms, and curricula for black students will continue to raise problems on campus for some time to come. Often colleges have come into conflict with federal civil rights laws because they gave in to black separatist demands.

The fourth, and historically a major cause of campus unrest, *is the Vietnam War*. The crisis occasioned by the breaking in of the draft on the lives of thousands of students has been quite severe. But it is more than the draft, for, after all, students were drafted in World

War II without such a crisis arising. Rather, it is the fact of being drafted into what many students and faculty consider an unnecessary and even immoral war that has literally set many campuses on fire. As the war heated up, so did the campus turmoil. As the war has wound down, so has campus unrest quieted.

The fifth cause of unrest is *the revolution in our youth culture itself*. The youth of today have interests, desires, and styles of life that differ radically from those of their parents. All in all, youth are radically different, even radically alienated, from the other generations around them. Students tell us that many modern youth are equally alienated from each other. This fact means that there are many, many issues on which the students and administration can "tear the blanket" and fall into dispute.

Glazer is very perceptive in locating the sixth root of campus unrest. He calls it *the crisis of authority*. It is quite true that not only the university but the nation as a whole is passing through a crisis of authority. This means that the foundations on which various authorities such as clergymen, policemen, judges, college presidents, and professors function are questioned. Of course, the authority of all these posts is not given in any absolute sense, except by the consensus of the people, and when the consensus is broken, there is social chaos. One can maintain *power* by force of arms, but one cannot maintain *"authority."* Authority is authority precisely because it does not rest solely on strength, but rests on acceptance and respect. Many people both young and old have lost their respect for the "authorities" on campus and in government in this country. Perhaps the only solution to this crisis is for those who occupy positions of authority to earn the respect of the people again.

If nothing else has been accomplished by this brief rehearsal of the campus movement, I hope the reader has gained the insight that the campus unrest of the recent past was not the result of adolescent foolishness or the plotting of Communist revolutionaries. Campus unrest is neither a lark nor a foreign plot. Rather, is is a serious, native problem brought on by the unresolved social tensions and political mistakes that we, the older generation, have either caused or allowed to continue.

There is, among the older and the conservative segment of our society, the belief that the breaking of any law or the infraction of any commandment (especially one dealing with sex) is inexcusable and that the offender must be punished. On the other hand, among many of our young people there is a counter belief rather inelegantly phrased for them by some of the Yippies, that smoking pot and free sexual expression in the streets are revolutionary acts. Perhaps the turn toward such self-indulgent "revolutionary" behavior on the campus helps explain the relative social "quiet" that has reigned recently in the United States. On the other hand, the turn toward such indulgence may be a mark of despair over the nonresponsiveness of society to youth desires.

Revolutionary Man as Sexually Liberated Man and Woman

In every radical publication of the last ten years and in most of the successful movies of the same period, one theme stands out clearly: the progressive man, the liberated woman, the person who has "had it" with the reactionary policies of the government, with the war in Asia and the repressive moral codes of middle America, is not only politically radical but sexually liberated as well. We briefly mentioned the connection of political consciousness, moral indignation, and sexual maturity in Chapter 1. We wish to deepen those insights here, since the revolution in sexual attitudes during the past decade has clearly influenced our view of what man is.

The theme of sexual liberation is deepened and broadened in many serious essays and books by America's most progressive thinkers and authors. Eldridge Cleaver writes of the black man who wants the black woman to be his queen. He writes of rape as a "revolutionary act"[5] and of the mystique of the "Super-Masculine Menial."[6] Norman Mailer, in blunt Anglo-Saxon terms, implies that conservatives are sexually repressed. To be "hung up" is a slang term that carries the psychological connotation of the repetition of past psychic (and physical) failures. This is the term that the young apply to both the political and the sexual beliefs of their elders.

I am constantly amazed and amused by the confluence of the themes of political-social radicalization and sexual freedom in the so-called "underground press." Reading the advertisements and the "classified ads" in *The Los Angeles Free Press*,[7] *The Great Speckled Bird*,[8] *The Village Voice*,[9] *The Blue-Tailed Fly*,[10] and similar papers is a liberal education even for a middle-aged man with war experience and fifteen years experience as a pastor and teacher. From the "want ads" we read in these papers we must conclude that radical people are very free indeed.

Compared to the writings and public statements of American radicals, the revolutionaries of other countries seem very Victorian. Even the romantic Cuban revolution with its men and women guerrilla fighters hiding out together in the mountains did not have the same sexual liberalism. Perhaps the influence of Marxism, with its nineteenth-century sexual negativism, is most seen in the Cuban revolutionaries' rule that punished men and women who slept together while in the hills. There is no such Marxist Victorianism in the new revolution of American black and white youth. Among the slang, slogans, poster-legends and writings of the New Left, sexual freedom has only two rival sources of symbols: astrology and drugs. The Age of Aquarius, as the new age is called by the young, is an age of full sexual expression, of mind expansion, of the "joyous conjunction of the planets," which is precisely why it is an age ready for a new form of society.

The implication of much of radical discourse is that if men and women were freer in expressing their sexual desires, and fulfilling them, we would all be more liberal and would create a more wholesome type of society. While this may be an oversimplification of reality (it is not an oversimplification of the radical thesis), it is still an insight that includes much truth. Repression, fear, and frustration in one area, especially in an area so basic as sex, leads to repression and fear in other areas as well. The person who is publicly squelched in self-expression undoubtedly has only two recourses in private life, to be repressed there also, or to overcompensate by throwing off all bonds on his conduct. Such a person may also plot, at least in fantasy, revolution.

The Precise Place of Sexuality in Social Radicalism

Although they overstress it, government agencies are not completely wrong in considering sexual delinquencies as indications of possible security risks. It is well known, and is now a moot legal issue, that homosexuals are not granted security clearances by "sensitive" government agencies. It is charged that the FBI has discharged agents for fornication, and enforces a Victorian code on all its employees. While some of these restrictions are ridiculous, the insight that people who experiment sexually are not the type of social conformists who will accept things as they are, on authority alone, is quite valid. The type of safe, conforming individual who makes the "ideal" government employee is the comfortably married, "straight" middle-class man. It is my observation that more young people become politically radical out of rejection of the life-frustrating (and hypocritical) sexual standards of America than out of an attraction to marijuana and drugs (which are also unrealistically persecuted). "In for a nickel, in for a dime," first free sex, then drugs, may very well be the first step in the process of the political radicalization of youth.

Since sexual freedom today so often involves group knowledge of what is going on, if not actual group sexual experience, this liberalization may also go along with exposure to "pot" and the more exotic drugs, such as LSD. Once this level of "outlaw" participation (for *any* experiment with "drugs," even with marijuana, which is *not* a drug, is illegal and is punished upon conviction) is reached, the rebellion of a youth against "the system" is fixed. Without the slightest political provocation—beyond suffering from social disapproval of natural sexual urges and seeing the police harassment of "pot smokers"—large numbers of youth are confirmed in "antiestablishment" attitudes. They become committed to what are, by definition, radical practices. Add an unpopular war, the frustration of international relations in a world of nuclear stalemate, racial unrest, and an uninspiring set of public leaders, and you have the raw materials for social explosion.

The Post-Modern Conception of Man

Down deep, below the image of man that informs the struggle for black pride, for full citizenship for migrant workers and Mexican-Americans, for political participation for young people, for the achievement of peace in the world, and for the abolition of poverty, lies one common theme: *Man is not someone that can be rationally understood, nor should he seek to understand himself and his world only on the rational level. Rather, man is one who feels, and only by feeling will we truly "grok," genuinely "know," ourselves, our fellows, and our world.* Immediate feeling and immediate response to that feeling is the only accepted way to truth on the part of large numbers of the young as well as by older nonconformists. "Please touch," "Lose your mind and come to your senses," are more than slogans. Now man must touch and feel the peculiar textures of the beings and things around him if he is to know and respond to the world. In the centuries-old struggle between the way of rationality and the way of irrationality, reason seems on the decline and the irrational seems triumphant.

Despair and Relativism

R. D. Laing has observed that despair is the sign of a man's frustration over believing in the existence of absolute values, while his everyday experience does not reveal such values as part of our society. I have long operated on a similar insight: that fundamentalistic beliefs, in religion or in politics, tend to disintegrate under the pressures of modern life. Once this occurs, a man is left morally cynical, and often an atheist. The person who starts out with high hopes is subject to fantastic social and psychological frustrations that can result in a premature and unrealistic sense of hopelessness. Our major moral and social problem in establishing a new and vital image of man today lies precisely in walking the tightrope between an unwarranted hope and a similarly unwarranted hopelessness. The chief signs of the crushed idealism and stillborn hopes of the current youth generation are *its continuing political quietism* and the continuance of violence by governmental agencies and private protesting groups in America.

I want to discuss some of the social and political ramifications of this hope-despair syndrome in the following sections. First, a discussion of violence,[11] then the possibility of seeing the Black Power movement as a form of humanism, and finally, the possibility of moving beyond many elements of the present-day life-styles of both middle America and the counter culture to the recovery of some elements of an older style of life that may be more human and satisfying than any now followed by the majority of people in the West. I want to present the thoughts of one man who has experimented, in his own life, with the possibility of recovering an older life-style in the interest of self-fulfillment and happiness. This man puts the question to us: "While thinking of new styles of life, why not think of the possibility of the reestablishment of an older one?" The "Back to the Land" movement among many ex-hippies and college students, the growing number of people of all ages who seem to be trying to *withdraw from our society,* making a separate peace with themselves and the world, leads me to believe that this idea of an older life-style may be very much up-to-date. It could be the key to "what's happening" right now. The popularity of *The Whole Earth Catalog,*[12] and the advice on communal living and group buying given in the radical journal *Ramparts,* tends to bear out the relevance of this, at first sight anachronistic, material.

Violence: Overt and Covert as a Major Thread of Modern Life

In order to appreciate fully the basic disillusionment of many youth with Western society, we have to be able to fathom the extent to which they are sensitive to the *covert* violence implicit in our culture. All age groups and political opinion types are aware of the *overt* violence endemic in American (and general Western) society. We share a common knowledge of our assorted murders, assaults, family fights, mass civilian killing in Vietnam, and street fighting in our cities. We differ from one another only on our opinions as to what the underlying causes of these violent acts really are. It is probably only the "McLuhan" generation,[13] reared in the all-embracing bath of the electronic media, with instantaneous news from every portion of the earth, however, that has become completely (even unconsciously) aware of the *covert* forms of violence that are structurally part of our civilization. These structures of covert violence remain hidden, invisible, until they surface in overt manifestations. (The analogy of the tip of the iceberg is very close here: men murder overtly only because covertly they hate, fear, and envy.)

Adults must recall that our present teen-agers have lived their entire lives under the spell of television. Most of their knowledge of the world has come to them via movies and programs on "the tube" rather than through books and/or the school and church. Much of what they have experienced through television has been heavily laced with symbols and literal descriptions of violence. An eighteen-year-old entering college has grown up on color coverage of the Vietnam War. The violence and suffering there have appeared in full color on the six o'clock news since 1961.

I do not intend to moralize about the content of television programs here. Studies have been made of the "violence level" of popular programs by experts in psychology and communications. I have already reported on some of these studies in a previous book.[14] What I want to stress here is the phenomenon of exposure to graphic depictions of violence from an early age among the members of the current youth generation. Such exposure has had *two distinct and opposite effects,* influencing young children in two diverse ways: (1) toward an interest in violence and a predilection for violent games, and eventually for service in war; and

(2) paradoxically, toward an absolute (or near absolute) rejection of violence. This reaction gives many young people a predilection toward passive life-styles and a resistance to (or outright refusal of) service in the armed forces. This paradoxical, double effect is a real phenomenon. It is being demonstrated by various young people we meet every day. It is explainable only in terms drawn from behavior therapy, i.e., in terms of *the reinforcement of previous conditioning* and of innate temperamental "styles" of coping with the world. This reinforcement is one of underscoring the general world view of the individual child. It is a personal reinforcement, one of the inner feelings of the child, and not only of his family and school influences. I say this because it is possible to point out two different effects on brothers reared in the same family. One comes to "appreciate violence"; the other grows to abhor it. What McLuhan, Reich, Roszak, and other commentators are trying to tell us is that "the second kind of brother" is becoming more common in our society. Reich's book, *The Greening of America*,[15] zeroes in on this rejection of violence as one of the primary elements in what he calls "Consciousness III."

The Signs of Violence

What are the signs of covert violence in our society that are picked up by those who are growing up with a "new mentality"? We can only list them here, but they include:

The continuance of forms and practices of racial discrimination, and the slowdown of the central government's efforts to dislodge these racist forms from their positions of power. Any form of ethnic or creedal discrimination is not only covert violence but is, when practiced, overt violence (so-called "police" or "legal" violence). Such misuses of justice can cause the reaction of violence on the part of those discriminated against, or else the growth of despair and a fall into drug abuse and other forms of self-destruction.

The continuance of the psychology of, and the forms and practices of, "The Cold War." The overallocation of natural resources and manpower to military purposes reveals the backbone of violence in American and Western (including Russian) society.

The growth of police and military surveillance of ordinary civilian activities in America. This practice serves to give many young (and older) people the feeling of being oppressed, if they are not actually oppressed by the central government.[16] Minimally, one becomes repressed in his free expression of social views by such operations.

The continuation of the military draft, in the face of its increasing lack of support from legislators, government officials, clergy, professors, teachers, peace groups, and millions of other sound citizens. On the other hand, the proposal to establish an all-volunteer army is not comforting, in the face of the traditional American belief that large standing armies are not to be regularly maintained.

The actual continuation of the Indochina war, and its spread, on American governmental initiative, to Cambodia and Laos (and Thailand and North Vietnam) *in spite of official declarations that the war is "winding down."* More than any other factor, the extension and escalation of this futile war, despite the fact that the majority of Americans want it ended, gives the average citizen a feeling of helplessness, of being ignored and thereby oppressed, in a supposedly democratic society by the Federal Government. Many people who are for peace say "The majority isn't silent; the government is deaf."

The growth in influence of right-wing groups in America, under the slogans: "Support Your Local Police"; "Law and Order"; and "The Silent Majority." Most right-wingers have felt freer to work and more socially "respectable" since 1968 than they have since the 1920's.

The "punishment" of public universities by state legislatures, and of private and church-related colleges by their supporters, through the reduction in funds and cutbacks in programs and staffs that have been the rule throughout 1971. Increasingly, state legislatures are taking steps to limit or do away with faculty tenure altogether. Never before has there been such a serious attack on the freedoms of speech and press. These moves can only be seen as an assault upon academic freedom. Such legislative procedures go hand in hand with the revelation that college students and their professors are under police surveillance in many instances. We are discovering that the political views and private statements of college people are taken down and kept in permanent (and secret) police, FBI, Secret Service, and Army files. The similarities of such governmental practices to those of Soviet Russia and Nazi Germany are real and disturbing to anyone who believes in democracy.

These, then, are some of the reasons why a growing number of Americans feel that ours is an increasingly oppressive society. Such concerned people feel that we need to adopt a new life-style, or to try several new life-styles, in the hope that they might help preserve the good things America stands for. Perhaps the good in our tradition can only be preserved in the birth of a new image of man in a new America.

Black Power as the Search for a Full Humanity

The raised fist of the Black Power advocate has become familiar to all in the past several years, yet when the term "Black Power" was first uttered, a shock went through both the white and the black communities. "Black Power" has been used in several widely varying senses. These different uses range from a call for a radical (and often revolutionary) Black Nationalism (among a *very* few), to a call for pride in one's Afro-American culture, to an attempt to give ego-support to thousands of blacks who have been psychically damaged by a lifetime of segregation and/or discrimination.

It seems that "Black Power" is many things to many people. However, the "mainline" tradition of Black Power appears to lie in the Black Panther party and in the revisionistic Black Muslimism of the followers of the late Malcolm X.

Black Panthers—A New Black Man

The newspapers have been filled with stories of esstranged relations with the white community on the part of Black Panthers (as well as Black Muslims who follow in the footsteps of Malcolm X and Eldridge Cleaver). These estrangements have often erupted into small wars. A number of Black Panthers have been killed by policemen, most often in police assaults upon Panther "headquarters." These meeting places have sometimes been converted into strongholds: sandbagged and supplied with weapons and ammunition. Some of the reports of such incidents suggest that the Panthers —admittedly armed, since they publicly advocate that black men should own arms—were not the instigators of these fire fights. Police departments have apparently been very nervous about and antagonistic toward the existence of a paramilitary organization such as the Panthers in the black ghetto areas of our larger cities. This is said, neither to defend the Panthers nor to attack the police, but simply to report the consensus of those who have investigated the matter.

"Black Power" for the Black Panther means a kind of aggressive black pride which not only expects but demands respect for the black man and woman, and a better social opportunity for black children. Such demands seem reasonable and warranted, considering American discrimination against blacks for so many centuries.

Black Power is "aggressive," however. Usually it is aggressive in a verbal, literary, and symbolical way. According to most investigators, Black Panthers are not known to be physically aggressive without provocation. While they affect a kind of youthful bluster and bravado, they are not known to assault ordinary citizens, white or black. Indeed, they live under a strict paramilitary, moralistic code that enjoins them *not* to become drunken, take dope, senselessly threaten others, or play around with firearms. The shoot-outs of Panthers and police have usually followed police raids on Panther members' apartments or Panther meeting places. Aggrieved by these raids, and full of "black pride," Panthers have then fought extended fire fights with heavily armed police units. Surprisingly few people have been killed in these pointless skirmishes. The police, with superior firepower and communications, plus better training and more experience, have invariably won. While some Panthers have been killed in these clashes, the majority of the members surrender after putting up a show of resistance sufficient to satisfy their pride. In these "battles" nobody really wins, for their very occurrence shows the complete breakdown of communication between governmental authority and radicalized blacks. For every Panther who falls, many young recruits, stirred by the example, come forward to swell Panther ranks. One cannot settle long-standing social problems by force, whether it be legally or illegally applied.

A moderate assessment of the Black Panthers would be that they are not genuinely dangerous revolutionaries. Nevertheless they form a cadre that could become revolutionary *if the polarization of American society continues,* and if we rely upon police power rather than upon human behavioral knowledge (social science) to attempt to solve our social problems. Treated with respect, and recognized as an inevitable result of the treatment that blacks have received in the United States, the Panthers could be turned into a constructive social force. They have already demonstrated this in their positive influence in the struggle against drug abuse among large, densely crowded black populations in our major cities. The free breakfast program run by the Panthers in some major cities in the East and on the West Coast are further examples of the constructive potential this movement toward a black form of humanism contains. It is up to the various governmental agencies and the religious organizations of America to attempt to cultivate this positive, constructive core in the Panther movement.

It would be well for all Americans to remember one truth: *No man can be a full man if he is inwardly or outwardly ashamed of his racial ancestry.* An Irish-American is a man and his Irish ancestry is a distinctive and attractive quality of his manhood. The same reasoning holds true for the German-American, the Scot, the Pole, the Frenchman, and for the man of Jewish descent. Why would we want to deny the same kind of ethnic pride to the man of African blood? Why should his pride in black manhood—and womanhood—be a threat to our white, or brown, or yellow manhood? Are we not all men, and *all* men, and all *man,* precisely because we have come into the world as unique individuals who nevertheless fall into various recognizable racial groups? If the black *man* cannot be a *black* man, then none of us can hope to reach the stature of full manhood. Black Power, even in its most socially frightening form, is an expression of humanism. We should learn not only to live with it, but to appreciate it. Only in such a spirit as this can Black Power make its unique contribution to the full development of a viable image of man.

A New-Old Life-Style [17]

The following assessment of life in the United States at present was made by a thoughtful man on the basis of his own experience. As we look at the changing life-styles around us, we need to keep in mind what this observer has to say, since he is reporting on a movement that is gaining popularity among both young and old today. The modern search for a new image of man seems to be based more on considerations of changes in life patterns than on the breaking of new philosophical ground. Our observer describes a return to a simpler form of life in this way:

While thinking of new life-styles, why not turn your attention to the reestablishment of an old one? Consider the life of independence and self-reliance. Naturally no man is an island, but no man is only a grain of sand on an island beach either. Self-reliance seems a virtue that has almost vanished in our time. While we would never have achieved the progress we have as a nation without the growth of interdependence, involving a surrender of some independence, we have now reached the state where we have almost given up the right to think for ourselves. In America we have turned over our right to think to advertising agencies, news commentators, and politicians. They try to tell us what to think, when to think and how to think. Those who would deviate from their opinions are sharply reprimanded or cunningly entrapped and brought back into line. If you don't believe this, look around you. Watch television for a while, attend to the advertisements, keeping in mind that they are trying to set you up.

Watch how skillfully they do it. If you don't use a certain soap, your wife will leave you. You won't get a raise if you don't spray something under your arms. One hundred twenty mile an hour cars are sold while our highway speeds are set at fifty-five and seventy miles an hour.

Listen to the news. All three networks report the same thing. Note where the accent is placed.[18]

Our individualist tells us that we cannot point to the hippie movement as a successful retreat from the mainstream of society. If we look at the ads on television and magazines, we see that the hippies have been swallowed up by business enterprises which ingeniously said, "If you can't lick them, join them." Businessmen have stopped trying to sell the hip young on their older world views and started to mass-produce hip clothing and artifacts. Now the person who doesn't dress in hip fashion is out of style. When I fly on airplanes, I find that most of the older businessmen are wearing sideburns and long hair, and some have moustaches and beards. Our books, television programs, and movies are full of "hip people." If one takes this preoccupation with "being hip" as an indication that the world has changed, he is wrong. One sees only the top of an iceberg, which means that the business community has turned another liability into an asset. Business know-how has turned social dropouts into come-ons for customers. It has turned free thought into another change of fashion, opening up a new consumer market. Business has had no change of heart but, driven by the profit motive, has manipulated the hippie movement to its own advantage.

Our cynical observer declares that business is not alone in this social ploy. "This same observation is true of the politicians who began some years ago to speak of peace and brotherhood. The political satire current in 1965-66 covers this phenomenon: 'They said that if I voted for Goldwater we would be at war in six months. I did and sure enough we were.' " [19]

Finding the Good Life

As we grow older, one of the most frequent topics of conversation is "the good old days." Liberals condemn conservatives for wanting to return to the past. But liberals seem to want to push us forward to the good new days as much as the conservatives want to hold us back. Neither group is wrong in this, for both want a better life-style than now exists. Yet both groups miss the point, for what the human being really wants lies at the fingertips of everyone.

Our individualistic friend further remarks:

Remember the good old days? Remember the fairy castles of your dreams? Those dreams were your memories of what it was to be a child when you had no great cares and responsibilities. Those dreams were not fulfilled by the New Deal, the Great Society or the civil rights movement, for what the human being wants is to be happy. How can anyone deny this? Mean people are mean because they are miserable with unhappiness. The mentally ill are ill because of unhappiness. But what makes us happy? Is it a new car that puts us in debt for three years? Is it a new house that puts us in debt for thirty years? The human being's answer should be "no," for what makes us happy is contentment. This is the root of our troubled society: there is no contentment in America. We produce more than other nations, our standard of living is higher, we are educated and emancipated but for all this we are the most unhappy and discontented people on earth.[20]

Why are Americans so apparently unhappy? Because we have been brainwashed into believing that civilization means automation. Perhaps we should remember that the Nazis were automated, but they were not, for all their science, civilized. Advertisements turn us away from our freedom to the living of imitation lives. Our freedom is taken away from us by the electronic environment, when we are given cues as to how we should "live" by the various social power groups.

Our society has been split in two, into the hip and radical on one side and the middle Americans on the other. Both groups are being exploited by business and the mass media since the movement for self-expression has been made a fad by Madison Avenue. Everything is make-believe; most of society's "mod people" are as plastic (false) as their parents. We live in a plastic world of plastic homes eating plastic food. Pop the precooked food into the oven and out comes a meal fit for our plastic tastes. The chief result of a public education is a population fixated on plastic substitutes for the real taste and feel of life.

Getting Wise to Being "Ripped Off" (i.e., Robbed)

Our worldly-wise informant next warns us against the dangers we face in being cheated, and tells of the freedom we gain when we learn to avoid such situations:

I have lived a tough life, seeing our society and several others from the bottom up. I had to learn to survive by using my mind, not by becoming a "con man" but by learning to make do and live on little or nothing. Basically, what I have learned in the past twenty years is the kind of thing that young people who are attempting to start communes are learning now.[21]

A Radical Style of Life: Communes

We have to face up to our feelings and inward image of ourselves. Therefore, we should consider the support, friendship, and family-like joy of an extended family—a commune. Many groups of Americans are setting up communes or co-ops today. Five or six families can pay for a large farm in a short time if they work together. When the bank is paid quickly the amount of interest paid is kept down. Even if none of the communal group is familiar with farming, this doesn't mean they cannot own a farm. There are many contract farmers in every rural area who will work the land for the nonfarmer. They offer several kinds of contracts, the easiest of which is one in which all the owner does is provide the land while the contract farmer provides everything else. One gets a very small percentage of the profit, but it is steady income and it takes no time or effort on the part of the landowner. This is what gentlemen farmers do; why can't people seeking an alternative life-style do the same?

Communism on a national level has never worked well, but on a lower, more personal level, entering into such an arrangement with people you like and trust can be quite successful. Actually, farmers in the United

States have used the communist principle successfully for many years in the co-op movement. The Mennonites, the Amish, the traditional Quakers, and other rural-based religious groups are founded on the co-op principle. Farming operations by these sects are said to be among the most successful in the world. The farmland around Lancaster, Pennsylvania, is rich and beautiful and is filled with sectarian co-op farms. Ohio, Indiana, the Dakotas, and many other states have similar groups.

Working together in a co-op will free everyone involved from the rat race of the nine-to-five job. It will give them leisure time to devote to their wives and children. It could provide the day-long base for the development of true friendship. It could lead one to a happier life. As Aristotle observed centuries ago, every man really aims at being happy.

Extending the Commune Principle

Once several communes have been formed in an area, they should begin to cooperate with each other for larger purposes. A group of communes might consider forming consumer clubs in which they pool their purchasing power, influencing retailers to lower their prices, either by refusing to buy from them, or by bribing them with the promise of all their business. After all, it is the retailers' claim that high-volume trade allows them to lower prices. The communes should use this principle to *their* own advantage. Another idea is for several communes to form a corporation, obtaining their own retail and/or wholesale licenses. This would completely eliminate the middleman and ensure more food and goods for less money. That is what farm co-ops do. The best way to break out of the economic rat race is by economic means. Such a "breakout" can be achieved legally, comparatively easily, and with a good deal of satisfaction. But such a move toward more freedom is possible only if one can motivate enough people to work together.

Being Aware of the "Rip-offs" in the System

Most people are cheated or "ripped off" (in the slang of modern youth) every day. Some of these "rip-offs" are so subtle that we are unaware of them. Occasionally they are not so subtle and we become vaguely upset because we think we have been cheated and can't prove it. One needs to make himself aware of the worst kinds of rip-offs and avoid them by making his own repairs and home improvements. Repairmen are often the economic downfall of the careless.

Almost everyone has made a purchase and found out later that he could have bought the item cheaper elsewhere. We have all purchased food and found it had no taste. Most of us have gotten angry because something we just bought broke down because of poor workmanship. Our economic system is full of such occurrences. Yet the person who would be economically free needs to avoid repairmen if at all possible.

While we do not want to say that all repairmen are dishonest, there is much overcharging, and charging for parts that have not really been replaced. Practices such as these give all repairmen a bad name. One needs to be particularly careful in having his automobile and his television set repaired. Unless one familiarizes himself with the various parts of these machines, he is at the mercy of the auto mechanic and the TV repairman. There are too many instances of parts being replaced when they did not need to be replaced, of charging for work that was not actually done, for anyone to feel secure when he has repair work done. The man who teaches himself some of the basics of repairing his own car and his television set is far ahead in the economic game. It is not impossible for anyone to gain a certain knowledge about the working of his automobile and his television set.

Our individualistic adviser offers the following advice. Strange to say, young children don't need this sort of advice, for they do what he suggests quite naturally.

The best defense against being ripped off is the offense of doing most of your own work. Why not watch what is going on when your equipment is being repaired? Why not buy some of the many do-it-yourself manuals that are available on every newsstand and in many supermarkets, that will help you to become self-sufficient? You can be more capable than you think you can if you take the time to inspect your equipment and study a few manuals. I have had excellent experience with manuals in a well-known series which contains books on plumbing, television repair, masonry, carpentry and other subjects. They sell for under $1.50 and are easy to read. People with but sixth-grade educations buy them, read them and do their own work. Couldn't you do the same? [22]

We can also become freer in our economic life-style if we think about little things. Let your hair grow. If you must have it neat, learn to trim it yourself. Clip off a little every morning; don't try to cut too much at once. In a few weeks you will be proficient. Considering the high costs of haircuts, a man can save a lot of money over the years by this simple practice.

If you don't smoke, don't start. If you do smoke, consider stopping. It will be good for your health if you do give up tobacco. If you don't want to stop smoking, consider buying a roll-your-own kit. Make your own smokes. Think about a pipe, which is less harmful to the health and less expensive. Liquor costs a great deal and does no one any real good. If you like a friendly drink or two, there is always beer. Beer is far cheaper than liquor and less hard on the body than wine. One can even buy a kit with which to make his own beer. Watch the magazine advertisements for an ad on a beer-making kit. Homemade beer tastes fine and usually costs less than a penny a bottle to make. Someone who made his own beer (in relatively small amounts) found that the cost of the cap on the bottle was more than the cost of the ingredients.

If you really want to change your life-style, information on how to do it is all around you. We only need to read about the tasks we want done and do something for ourselves for a change.

Perhaps all of us need to remember something the college student learns in his student days and regularly seems to forget when he graduates. It is the message that the poor in every country, in every time, give us when we talk to them. That message is: you have to be smarter to be "poor" than to be "well off." Life cannot be taken for granted when one lives in an alternative way from the middle-class norm in America. If one chooses to go back to the land, to drop out of the race for success, he will have to use his mind and hands. One has to consider every angle just to survive.

This consideration of every detail in life is what our great-great-grandfathers knew when they were pioneers and settlers. This is the wisdom of the life-style of the American Indian who roamed over the country freely, living off the land. One has to keep one step ahead of events, for when one cuts himself off from the security that goes with the bondage of institutions, disaster is always only one step away. Yet everything you learn to do for yourself, every way you learn to lower your living expenses, is the cutting of another web of your bondage to the plastic life of the status quo.

Our proponent of a new-old life-style concludes:

Just think of it—free from the need of keeping up a front. No longer worried about what other people think, but about what you think and your friends think about your life-style. You will still need to work to earn a living but you can limit yourself to work you don't have to take home. Such a life-style will not be a utopia, for no one can offer you perfection. It isn't even really a new life-style, but the reestablishment of an old one. This is the way of the pioneers, the life rural old folks will tell you about if you visit them. It is the style of life in which everyone helped everyone else. It was a way of living that lacked the mental pressures we have built into the modern world. It rips away the pressure of materialism and makes it possible for us to live like human beings again. It substitutes happiness for success, but it seems to me that happiness is to be preferred over successful unhappiness in any sensible life.[23]

Understanding Life-Styles as Attempts to Be Truly Human

Perhaps the brief excursions through various alternative life-styles that we have taken so far in this book are surprising. Such a survey may confirm some in their opinion that ours is a "revolutionary period." *Where one is himself will determine how he reacts to the variety of experiments in living that are the inner history of our time.* Whether one accepts or rejects any one or all of these experiments matters less, however, than does his honest attempt to realize the spiritual agony in the lives of millions today. When one is able to see such alternative life-styles in the late twentieth century as attempts of troubled people to become more truly human in a largely dehumanized society, he is halfway to becoming more human himself.

Chapter 4

LIFE-STYLES—
THE INFORMED AND CONFORMED

In a remarkable term paper for one of my courses, a freshman co-ed summed up the philosophy and changed life-styles of modern youth. Entitling her paper "Where do we go—flow with the river? Where do we go—follow the Sun?" she observes:

Mankind is forever involved in the making of decisions. These will determine whether he becomes a truly released individual whose creative spark has been nurtured, or an individual who follows a rather preplanned life schedule where creativity is developed only if needed or useful. Parents may urge children to "be something"—possibly they equate this with standards that may or may not apply to the child. The conflict arises when the child begins to think on his own.

It is a fairly common fact that people find security within patterns of life that reflect what they feel and which do not cause them to change very much. So, these people form a huge mass that drifts along like a river: This river only empties into larger bodies of water where it melts into the immense anonymity of the ocean; as people melt into a sameness—a fluid transparency that allows those not in the river to easily see through them, and to encounter difficulty in distinguishing them from one another.[1]

Such alert young people observe that people in our culture spend more time making material choices than they do in determining their values in life. Thus many in America pursue false values, or lose themselves in the river of conformity. In the river we are always in a hurry, and yet we run because we are frightened by the sheer foolishness and senselessness of what we are doing. In following the steps so clearly marked out for us by school, government, and business we may soon come to feel that things must be right if everyone is doing it. As the young student says:

> The problem in going along with the crowd is that it only offers answers we already know and expect. They do not make us face up to what we are honestly like. They stifle us, leaving no room for creativity. The pathetic reality, though, is that conformity and people who are like us "kill our souls." They afford us no room for challenge and discovery of new ideas. We become too one-sided and narrow-minded. This leads us to filling our days and lives with trivia which is evidence of the meaninglessness eating away at our souls.

With no inner direction and strength, we are people helplessly carried along with the river. In the phraseology of the hippies, we are becoming "plastic." [2]

Being Aware of Our Plasticity

In an earlier book,[3] I discussed the difference between the thinking of this current generation and that of older generations. I pointed out that the element of self-awareness—in the larger sense of being aware of what we are because of the history that lies behind us—is determinative for the new mentality of modern youth.

Recently my thesis that there is a new mentality has received support from Charles A. Reich, of Yale University, in his best-selling book, *The Greening of America*.[4] Reich speaks of three levels of consciousness: Consciousness I, a stress on nineteenth-century values, which is the loss of the sense of reality that seems common in our day; Consciousness II, which is formal and logical and plans ahead, creating the corporate state; and Consciousness III, which is the world outlook of the younger generation that concentrates on the development of self and interpersonal relations. Reich's Consciousness III is almost identical with what I have called the new mentality. As I expressed the content of this new mentality, it is essentially a reemphasis on the value of persons as persons and a recovery of feelings and sensations that put one in touch with reality. I observe that young people are not in revolt—it is far more basic than that! Their conduct is the logical expression of new ideas and new values becoming current. The beatniks, the peaceniks, the hippies, and the concerned students in the universities are expressing in different ways a sweeping international shift in man's concept of himself and the world.

Another student of mine, commenting on his experience of viewing the National Film Board of Canada's film *Prologue,* expressed the strong passive element in the new mentality in these words:

The practice of one's beliefs easily invites ethical compromise in proportion to the "radical" nature of those beliefs. It is a type of moral warfare; victory is approached by imposing moral compromise upon the opponent, hopefully in a subtle enough manner that he never suspects the bargain.

On the left, there seem to be two actions: (1) demonstration and revolt against the "opposition," and (2) withdrawal from the "war" as completely as possible into "communes" of moral example. The latter of the two practices reminds us of Thoreau's *Walden* ideal. Certainly revolt leads to tremendous frustration, especially against a power-based system such as ours. Whereas to serve one's beliefs by merely exemplifying full-time (without time off for confrontation) those beliefs is bound to be more personally fulfilling, and void of compromise. Confrontation invites forced compromise; often necessitating it. If the terms are reduced to force and submission the outcome will inevitably favor the mighty.

As rational discourse seems capable of serving as impetus to social change these days, the survival of any belief depends more heavily upon its manifest example than the "defenders of the faith." An army is an army is an army. Peace is better.[5]

Reich observes that Consciousness III starts with the self as the only reality. It is a philosophy that emphasizes living every moment. Yet this is not selfishness, for Consciousness III or the new mentality postulates the supreme worth of all selves regardless of race, creed, color, or political belief. It is this interpersonal value, as well as the value of one's own person, that leads many students to embrace the peace movement and resist the draft. The clarity of vision of these strange new people is terrifying. With sharp eyes they see through all the propaganda about free enterprise and open opportunity.

With a kind of modern monasticism they identify themselves with the poor, the black, the hungry. In many respects the young person who has dropped out of school and gone on the bum is like the ancient philosopher Diogenes.

Diogenes was a protester and scandal-making freak in his day. He went from place to place carrying a lighted lamp instead of a guitar, insultingly declaring that he was searching for someone who could be called a man. Settling down in a city, he lived in a tub in the marketplace. Almost naked, he had only his begging cup, tub, and lamp. Like the hippies who go to the country to form communes, Diogenes wanted to see how much he could do without, in contrast to his society, which placed emphasis upon consumption. After seeing a man form a drinking cup out of his hands, Diogenes even threw away his cup.

One of my students, remarking upon her affection for the figure of Diogenes, wrote:

Alexander the Great came to Athens and went down to the marketplace to see Diogenes; as he was about to leave he asked, "Is there anything I can do for you?" "Yes," Diogenes said, "you can get out of my light." The things a man can do without! There was nothing Alexander could do for Diogenes but move aside and let the sunlight fall upon him. Diogenes had learned that which is real in the world; so that he could no longer be tipped or bribed with what the world thought reality but what he saw as illusion. He had remained in his place, the place of wisdom, and had put Alexander in his place—of power.

Diogenes could tell us that we are not willing to labor to be wise; we are not even willing to be wise.

It would be a change, and we are not willing to change; it would make us different from other Americans and we are not willing to be different from them in any way.[6]

Heeding the Call

On every hand rock music holds out to us the images and feelings of those who have become "cool" or aware of reality. In trying to describe what moving from the older form of consciousness to the newer form of consciousness is like, I am unable to come up with any original terms. Conversion is an old-fashioned word, and yet it seems that it is the only proper term. Conversion from an older form of consciousness that maintains itself by never fully feeling the weight of one's own body and the brevity of one's own lifetime, the bittersweetness of the loneliness of other people and their need of us. Conversion to a feeling of oneness with others and the totality of things that exist, to a commitment to let peace begin with me, to a commitment to a new mankind, even if the number of those who are truly new is relatively small and powerless.

Yet the emphasis upon inwardness and the concern for self must be seen as the underpinning for a concern for everyone, or it merely becomes the selfishness that is so much a part of the older forms of mentality. A bearer of the old mentality very often feels sorry for himself. He may be unconcerned about the plight of the blacks in the ghetto or of the continuing suffering in Indochina but extremely concerned about his own bank account and the fact that he is losing his hair. This is

LIFE-STYLES—THE INFORMED AND CONFORMED 95

not the kind of concern for self that we are talking of. Rather, we are talking about the concern that by simply fitting in and adjusting to the system we will miss the fulfillment of our lives and thus give up any chance to be of service to humanity as a whole.

To the bearer of the new mentality, the old mentality, particularly the kind of well-adjusted personality that fits into the demands of the university and the business corporation, the government and the military, is a simple schizophrenic reaction. It is not normal or healthily human, for it is a retreat from anxiety-arousing stress to a lower level of psychological functioning that involves emotional indifference to others and lowered aspirations for mankind. It is a substitute of economic and household security for the thrill and risk of being fully human. It is a cop-out, an act of cowardice, if one is even vaguely self-aware, or of incredible ignorance when one is not.

The Revival of Religion Among Members of the New Mentality

One has only to listen to the rock music favored by the student generation to hear the name of Jesus Christ, of Buddha, of Krishna, mentioned over and over again. In some way many modern youth identify their new mentality with the kind of teachings and life-styles exhibited by the great religious and philosophical teachers of the past.

The rock opera *Jesus Christ Superstar* [7] puts the new mentality of the founder of Christianity squarely before us. Jesus is represented as a man different from others, because he sees through the cruelty and the enjoyment of power of the men around him. Even the apostles are represented as being interested in writing the Gospels so that they would be remembered after they were dead. Jesus, on the other hand, even in the context of the giving of the Last Supper, is shown to be unsure as to whether he will be remembered ten minutes after he is dead. The text of the opera is biting in its honesty, but nowhere is it blasphemous.

The significance of Jesus Christ for one young person can be seen in the following description of freedom and true selfhood:

There is a lot of talk going around today on freedom. Some people are at least defining freedom in terms of personal responsibility and direction, rather than with the idea that encases freedom as something which some countries have and some don't. Freedom exists in the mind. . . . "Don't you know that you are free, well, at least in your mind, if you want to be." Freedom only exists where things are "loose and elastic," so there is room to grow. People are not free today because they are slaves to themselves, and they don't realize that they can break away. Malcolm Boyd, an Episcopalian minister, candidly admits that, like most of us, he is a "captive to myself." Spinoza says to be ourselves, we must complete ourselves, and Socrates' famous words were, "Know thyself." Ralph Waldo Emerson implores us to "Trust thyself." But before we are ready to complete ourselves, we run from ourselves. . . .

Jesus puts it beautifully when he states that we are to be as free as the birds and so uncluttered that we should "therefore take no thought for the morrow." This is all we would have to do, but we make it too hard. We often live in a hell of our own making.

We may say we want a new leader, but that is not what we really want. What we want is a Messiah who will give us the word that is agreeable to us, that appeals to our preferences and prejudices, so that we can follow it wholeheartedly. But this is not what a true leader does. A leader tells us what we ought to hear, not what we want to hear. This is the difference between a false messiah and a true one. A false messiah—such as Hitler—caters to and inflames our fears, hates, angers and resentments. A true messiah—such as Jesus—rebukes us, shows us our errors, makes us want to be better, and asks us to make sacrifices for the common good and for the good of our own souls. He is never followed by every man, often is killed by the majority. All the true prophets make us feel worse. They knew and said that the trouble wasn't with our enemies, but with ourselves. They demanded that we shed our old skin, and become New Men. This is the last thing we want to do. What we are looking for is a leader who will show us how to be the same old men, only more successfully.

The great prophets were not paid by the religious community. They were actively opposed in most cases by the religious establishment. The false prophets who told the people what they wanted to hear were paid by the religious community. . . . The prophets wrote largely in poetry. It is possible that they even put their poetry to music and sang the message. . . . They even used demonstrations in the street to bring the message home. Isaiah went through the streets naked for three years. Jesus' most effective teaching was done through public demonstration. . . .

"Some may come and some may go, He (Christ) was surely best." [8]

Analysis and Reflection

In reflecting upon the Christmas season celebrations held in his large Midwestern parish, a sensitive younger pastor who shares the consciousness of youth describes what a depressing effect the "spirituality" of the old mentality can have on one who possesses "Consciousness III." For him, Christ and "Christmas" can have no meaning apart from real efforts to find genuine peace *in this world*.

The period after Christmas each year is always a low point in the life of any pastor. First, there is an emotional letdown which normally follows the hectic pace of the Christmas season. But more important, there is that gnawing feeling of frustration that even though we have boldly proclaimed the arrival of the "Prince of Peace" as a sign of God's love and concern for all mankind, the proclamation has once again fallen on deaf ears. It didn't really make any difference, did it? PEACE—LOVE—CONCERN. A bunch of idealistic dreams to give preachers something to talk about. But that season is over now. Back to business as usual. WAR —GREED—HATE.

So year after year, and again this year, we have spoken of the possibility of peace and love as if we had them, when in effect we have never seriously expected them. And rather than having Christmas a celebration of the birth of the "Prince of Peace," we have made it our principal annual orgy of innocence, which is really hypocrisy and even blasphemy.

Observing that much of our traditional religious outlook focuses upon "otherworldly" or ancient events, effectively leaving the people and problems of today completely out, the young minister goes on to say:

> Like people who cram everything into closets and drawers when unexpected company rings the bell, our kind of Christmas sweeps everyone out of sight and therefore out of trouble—at least as far as we're concerned. Christmas is as one person described it, "our unique depopulation bomb."
>
> But anyone who knows anything about the Scriptures knows that this isn't how it was at all. Or at least, they should know. For the event which we call the Incarnation was God's way of saying to you and me that "Where people are, that's where I live. When you want me, knock at the door behind which you hear the sounds of sorrow or the silence of loneliness. Where there is despair, look for me there. Find a brother and there you will find me."
>
> You see, it is absolutely imperative that you and I understand that Christmas didn't take people out of things. Christmas, to the contrary, said that people are what it's all about. Is it any wonder, then, that you and I haven't done a very good job of living the peace we pay lip-service to when we've tried so hard to take the people out? We've covered with a gigantic snow job the season most dedicated to people.
>
> Peace will come, if it comes, not only bumper to bumper but father to daughter or son, husband to wife, child to parent. Close to home, peace is sometimes the most elusive peace of all. It will not come without respect for personhood. One of the tragedies of our time is that when we subconsciously dream up an idyllic Christmas peace, those who are biologically closest to us may not be in the picture at all.

The author of these remarks asks how peace is to be achieved in the context of our present culture religion? How do we ever get to the point where we feel as secure, as carefree, in the peopled places of life as we do in the unpeopled places?

Maybe it's only when we start making Christmas cards out of slums, and battlefields, and starving kids. If we moved it back so it touched the real crisis areas of our lives, the results would be . . . perhaps PEACE—and LOVE—and CONCERN—toward all mankind. . . .[9]

A World Outlook Shared by Old as Well as Young

The similarities of sentiment between this pastor (in his middle thirties) and the feelings of both male and female undergraduates quoted earlier reveal the transcendent nature of the new mentality—the appearance of a new man. The forms and depths of feelings that make up the life-style of this generation cut across every barrier, including age. Talking to such people, if you are one yourself, is like meeting someone from home who speaks your native language when traveling in a foreign land. Perhaps the deliberate spelling of "America" as "Amerika" by some of the disillusioned young demonstrates this feeling of being in a strange land even here at home, better than any explanation can do.

In all those who are vitally concerned with the spiritual or religious issues today, there seems to be a feeling something like that which I once expressed in a "homemade" campus liturgy:

> To whom can we turn
> but to Jesus?

> And where can we find
> Jesus but among men?
> The Man for others
> Is the Man in Man
> Revealed in the kind Man
> Among mankind.[10]

And the manner of coming to this appreciation of "Jesus," or to this "conversion," is at once highly personal and completely social. As our "liturgy" went on to say:

> Not in the dark, nor in the deep
> Not in a vision nor in sleep
> Not with external show of power
> But there within the average hour
> There in the nexus intertwined
> Person to person together
> There in a moment within time
>
> There within reason
> In its due season
> Happens the miracle—The New Being
> Which will kill
> The old man within us.
>
> Thus does the Spirit feed
> Man's spirit at its point of need:
> Healing an estranged race
> By the pharmacology of grace.[11]

Metanoia

The emphasis on "conversion" among the mystically-minded young is seen among the "Hare Krishna" groups that sing and chant on the streets of Boston, Philadelphia, and every other large city, as well as among the Sino-American Buddhists of San Francisco and the new "Jesus People." *Look* magazine has offered a full photo story of the revivalistic movement that is half-humorously called the "Jesus Freaks." A "freak," of course, means a person "turned on" to something, usually drugs, but one can also be turned on to music, religion, or other activities. To be a freak means to be utterly consumed by some interest or activity. For the Jesus Freak, the interest is the old-time religion about Jesus; in theological terms, the practice of the presence of God through Christ.

The *Look* magazine [12] photo essay on the Jesus Freak movement of California demonstrated the size and vitality of such an appeal to youth in the 1970's. Hundreds of young people, many of whom once experimented with drugs or rode souped-up motorbikes wildly through the streets, now waded out into the Pacific to be baptized and to be "born again." Some of the "converts" reported the great joy that filled them when they accepted this old-fashioned gospel of personal salvation. They seem happy now, and confident about the future in ways that they have never felt confidence before. They have, in their way, turned from "flowing with the river" of conformity to the standard practices of alienated youth, toward "following the sun" of a responsible life of loving, personal service to other people. For these kids, God is not dead in any sense, for they are convinced of the living power of his Spirit at work in them.

Carl Braaten, a Lutheran theologian, tells us that the loss of faith in the ancient Christian eschatological hope

—the faith and hope that God will do something great in the future—led to the belief that God is dead. But that time of lack of hope seems past for the Jesus Freak. He is full of hope, and confident that Christ is here now and will return triumphantly in the future.

As one student seeker in religion declares:

And we move on in search of light
Light that is not something which we manufacture in our entangled mind—
but light which displaces all the falsities and errors and overwhelms
me with such intensity of surfaces and deepness
. . . . And we move on in search of light.[13]

How can one be at all perceptive and fail to see that *salvation*—in the mystically religious, far more than in the social gospel sense—*is the theme of our generation?* What, after all, is the content of the songs young people sing and "groove" to? Doesn't Paul Simon declare that Jesus loves even Mrs. Robinson, the aging seducer of young boys? The lyrics declare, over and over, that Jesus hears us when we pray. And even in the hardest of the acid rock tunes, the struggle between the good vibrations of Jesus or God and the destructive vibrations of the devil is represented by both words and music. They ask us what on earth, in heaven or in hell, were Janis Joplin and Jimi Hendrix after? Those who sing and those who listen to rock music have had the experience of drugs many times—which, bad as they might be, don't have to kill one quickly unless one is careless or doesn't care.

The Way of the Commune

The search for salvation among the young has taken on an institutional form in the experiments with communes among younger people, in California, Arizona, Washington State, and in scattered locations all over the United States and Canada.

The film *One Step Away* presents as accurate and impartial a picture of the communal attempt as we are likely to have on film. The good and the bad points of young people living in the open, raising children while smoking marijuana and hitchhiking about, are brought out in the story. The lack of both shelter and good food, as well as the abundance of exercise and fresh air, is presented without judgment. The attempts to relate to each other under new, experimental forms, without marriage and outside the law, are given without special pleading for or against. One hippie mother declares in the film, "You should never give a child acid (LSD) until he's eight years old and then only if he asks for it." Only the fact that an older man is also present, giving arguments against such attitudes, prevents the film from becoming ridiculous at that point.

One Step Away seeks to study the leader of a California commune. As the movie opens, a communal experiment located some 122 miles north of San Francisco is breaking up. The film follows the former leader and his "woman," giving us a vision of what life was actually like in Haight-Ashbury. Hippie families are shown "toking up" on marijuana, blowing the smoke into the faces of their infants so that the children too can get "stoned" (intoxicated). The leader is shown bringing another "chick" (girl) into the same "pad" (apartment) with his "wife," without regard to her feelings on the matter. The lack of contact with reality that characterizes all these group members is clearly presented. People talk "by" each other, not "to" each other. Yet, at times, when a group member is in depression, the other members do gather around and try to help him or her with comfort and large doses of the "hippie philosophy." But, hanging over all the action is the basic insight that the hippie trip is dead. "People think we are in hell, but we're in heaven," the leader says, but they are really only one step away from illness and/or death.

A "Hip" Co-ed's Reaction

One co-ed after viewing the film *One Step Away* had the following reaction:

I felt that the main people in *One Step Away* (the family) were in the minority inside a minority.

They didn't seem to know "where they were or where they were going." Sometime in the future they might be able to get their stuff together, but at the rate they're going it will take them about the same amount of time that it took the children of Israel to reach Canaan's land.

I don't think that they were really happy living the way they lived. When Harry made out with Leslie in front of his wife, Ricky, he showed that he really didn't love Ricky. (But then I don't think he really cared about Leslie either.) Harry, I'm sure, has a lot of internal hang-ups, and uncertainty about a lot of things.

Ricky seemed to be quite young. She might have been

able to get her stuff together better if she had had someone to help her. It seemed that she really cared about Harry. (She was hurt when he went with Leslie.) But he didn't feel the same about her. Also I think she loved her baby, but I couldn't understand why she treated him the way she did—blowing smoke in his face. Little babies are naturally stoned, so she didn't need to do that. Also he was pretty dirty most of the time and only wore a top; this doesn't seem like a very healthy environment. If the parents are messed up, think how messed up the kid is going to be . . . acid at 8 years.

Although I wouldn't pay to go see this movie, it did show me something. It showed me what I don't want to become.[14]

The Hippie's Search for a New Humanity

One of the great poets of our generation, Paul Simon, has told us that the words of the prophets are written on the subway walls. It certainly does seem true that the wisdom of our rising new generation comes across on buttons, bumper stickers, and graffiti written on every available surface. Many of these slogans declare that something or other is dead. My observations lead me to an opposite conclusion. I believe something is very much alive now, but may be in danger of death—the human freedom to be different.

Our generation seems to be one that has a single, incontrovertible response to every topic whatsoever—It's dead! We have been told that God is dead, reason is dead, even that sex is dead. Yet, unless we cannot see what's going on around us, we must be impressed by the Jesus Freaks, for whom God is certainly not dead, as well as by the more traditionally religious who unconcernedly go on singing and praying. By the same signs, we see the American flag sewn on everything from the shoulders of policemen to the bottoms of co-eds' jeans. Patriotism is a live topic in the 1970's, to say the least. While the university seems somewhat wounded, it is still alive enough to be raising its tuition; and if we pass the heavy shrubbery on campus, we will come away convinced that sex is not completely dead. We say this because it is widely believed that the hippie is dead. In some degree, if we think of the East Village and the Haight-Ashbury district, the hippie movement may be past, but like nationalism and sex, hipness is not something that dies on the spot when told it is dead by *Time* magazine.

The "liveness" of the hip style of life is shown by the content of many recent films. We need to consider these films as comments on the current social scene. They include *Medium Cool, Easy Rider, Prologue* (by the National Film Board of Canada), and *One Step Away*. We might also include in this category *Woodstock, Alice's Restaurant, The Strawberry Statement, Joe, Getting Straight,* and *Homer*. The hippie is as popular in films today as the American Indian—a parallel that is not without some significance.

Mentalities and States of Consciousness

> We are named by the things
> We will never understand.
> —*LeRoi Jones.*

We have all experienced, or can experience very simply by going to a cinema, the manner in which the hippie is presented by the mass media. He is presented as the alienated from general society, the breaker of taboos. If there are any areas of life that still rate being called "taboos" in the anthropological sense, then uncleanliness, promiscuous sexuality, and drug intoxication must be twentieth-century taboos. Consequently, the hippie, like the outsider in a French existentialist novel or play, is presented as an unfastidious, sexually free, pot-smoking person—or unperson. It really doesn't matter whether the book or article or movie is written by someone sympathetic to the hippie or antagonistic to him—these characteristics occur over and over. That wearing one's clothing till it is rather grimy, sleeping around, and smoking pot are as characteristic of soldiers and young people in general as of hippies doesn't seem to sink into the public consciousness.

I want to discuss the hippie as presented especially in films, while giving a social-psychological analysis of the current national scene. We also need to correct some analyses made by Charles Reich in *The Greening of America*.[15] I feel qualified to do this, since I first published the thesis that we have a confrontation today between two states of consciousness in *The New Mentality*,[16] more than a year and a half before Reich's book appeared.

"A New Humanity?"

> A soldier with no zest for fighting
> A poet with no zeal for writing
> An architect without a plan
> Is the hippie real or a plastic man? [17]

In my opinion, the hippie must be viewed from the standpoint of social psychology, as a representative type of human response to the peculiar challenges and threats of our day. The hip man and woman represent a mode of being-in-the-world, a psychic approach to existence that reveals itself in a unique life-style that sets theirs apart from other modes of consciousness. The genuinely hip person is hip, then, on the inside, and the exterior ornamentation or lack of it is accidental. That this modality of being usually ushers in a lack of uptightness about neatness and dirt, about the niceness of legal distinctions in sexual expression, and a relaxed attitude toward marijuana and drugs may be true, but one can have all these unsocial characteristics and still not be a hippie. Conversely, one can bathe daily (as most hip people do when it's possible, anyhow), be faithful to one other person and never smoke dope, and be more hip than Tom Wolfe or Ken Kesey. The world is full of plastic people (or pretenders) and the streets are full of plastic teenyboppers and weekend hippies, as anyone who lives near Harvard Square, The Village, The Haight, or the West Bank in the Twin Cities knows. We must go beneath the freaky clothes and the army patches if we are to find the real hippie. In the last analysis, that is part of the message of *Prologue* and the reverse side of the message of *Medium Cool*. (Although the condemnation of the straight society as seen at the Chicago riots in 1968 is the main story line in both films, the analysis of who is really hip is the undertheme in both also.)

To be distinguished as different, a thing must have some integral characteristics. It must have some qualities that set it apart from other similar but different things. In the case of men, we often get hung up on exterior characteristics, making mistakes that no zoologist would make about an animal species. Just how do we define the hippie? I proceed by analogy.

The Hippie and the Indian

In the high Andes, on the Peruvian-Bolivian border, near Lake Titicaca, are found the Aymara Indians. Living two and one half miles above sea level, these Indians have developed into a unique species of man. In many respects they show the same characteristics as the hippies of twentieth-century America. They are carefree, live wrapped in myths, have no money or power, use dope, are peaceful and humble, and seem very close to nature. They are colorful, compared to the city dwellers of the world, but their life is hard, and while they enjoy every moment of every day, their lives are short and their culture makes no progress. No one is going anywhere, and yet, while Inca and Spaniard pass away, these Indians endure.[18]

The Aymara Indian differs from other men not only in language, work habits, and clothing; he differs internally, in the clearest way. The Aymara have larger hearts, lungs, spleens, and livers than other men, because their bodies have adapted themselves to the high altitudes of the Andes. But equally profoundly, they, like the Eskimos, have adapted themselves to *survival without progress, to an immanent transcendence that leaves anxiety about the future quite out of mind.* The hippies I know seem more like Aymara Indians than like their older brothers and sisters. Even the enlarged liver of the habitual pot smoker forms a parallel. Yet, I mean this only as a literary, not a medical or scientific, analogy.

What makes a mountain Indian different from a lowland man? It is not just the manner of life, it is not the food he eats, the clothes he wears; rather, the difference between various life-styles is the total sum of the reactions of the individual man to his environment and to the challenges and the opportunities that his life situation affords him. We all know that this means that in a hot climate man will wear clothing that is cooler, and in a cold climate he will find a way to keep warm. But these things are the topics of anthropology, and we are more interested in approaching the hippie from the philosophical and psychological side. Looked at in this way, we see the basic response of a human being to his time and place.

Middle-class morals, or their rejection, and types of dress, food, work, and play follow naturally from the style of thinking that human beings adopt because of what they are and what they experience. The difference between the mountain tribesman of New Guinea and the city dweller of New York is one of mind, much more than of the way he comports himself in making a living. This is an existential way of looking at things. Classical Marxism holds that the way a man earns his living causes him to think in certain ways. *I suggest that it is because we think in certain ways that we choose to live the way we do.* How man thinks determines his world and how he will comport himself. If we see the world from some recessive, childish, selfish perspective, we will make great businessmen, and profits, savings, and security will be interesting to us. On the other hand, if we see the world as a total bundle of life, we will not put away for the future and we can live only prodigally. We cannot live destructively, tearing down, but we will live consumptively. Like the wild animals, we will eat what we need and leave the rest alone.

There are many social and psychological analyses of our age: some Marxist; some capitalist. There is also the analysis of fundamentalist religion. Against all these I would set the kind of analysis I do in *The New Mentality* [19] and Charles Reich does in *The Greening of America*.[20] I have tried to make a distinction between the old mentality of the pre-1960's and the new mentality of the past decade. This new thought-world of the new man also involves other styles of living, which take cues from Oriental sources, from primitive Christianity and American Indian sources. If one takes cues from Buddhism, from the Maharishi Mahesh Yogi, from Thomas Merton, and from the Indians of the Great Plains and mixes them together, one has the new mentality. Other "new" people take cues from nineteenth-century revivalism and become Jesus Freaks. They have a new mentality too. All these are bearers of a new humanity to us and to others who share in it. Today there are also the new fugitives, the exiles from the draft and the war who have deserted the country to go to Denmark and Canada. Others have retreated to living on farms and attempting to go back to nature. These too share the new mentality. To the "hardhats" they are all "hippies," but they are *not* all the same kind of people.

LIFE-STYLES—THE INFORMED AND CONFORMED   113

Activistic Young People

There is another large subdivision in this life-style, the group of political activists. They are not all hippies, for some are priests or men who were going to be priests. These are men who have looked into the future and seen only dullness and tragedy, for they believe that the price of our civilization is too high for human beings to pay. These men share the new mentality also. Actually, the activist is not the same as the hippie, but forms type A of the new mentality, of which the hippie is type B.

Charles A. Reich has carried this analysis of states of consciousness farther and divided the old mentality into two parts, Consciousness I and II. *Medium Cool, Easy Rider, Prologue, One Step Away,* and other films present the struggle between these three forms of human consciousness. There are two forms of consciousness (I and II) that are "not with it." Both of these forms of consciousness are fashions in which men have tried to come to grips with life in the past. Both of them represent unrealistic psychological reactions to our situation when looked at from the side of today's problems.

The first form of the old mentality is Consciousness I.[21] This is the belief that if you are a good boy, go to school, wash behind your ears, have a paper route, and go to a university, you will have your reward. God will not let him suffer who has worked hard. This is an example of what Richard Nixon felt—the Horatio Alger myth. The probable reason why Richard Nixon was a bitter man after his unsuccessful bid for governor of California was that he couldn't figure out why he was defeated. He couldn't understand why his disciplined efforts didn't work. It is the myth which the old American dream tells us made the world work. The fact that Daniel Boone couldn't keep a deed recorded in a county courthouse in Kentucky (because of political chicanery) and died in poverty shows us that Consciousness I was only a myth. It is a myth that died a flaming death in the Great Depression, although many people have not yet heard of its death.

The second form of older consciousness Reich calls Consciousness II. Consciousness II is the myth of the organization man. It is the myth against which students have rebelled on many campuses, sometimes to the point of violence. It is the state of consciousness of those who see that the modern world is amenable only to united effort. This form of thought built the Social Security system, the Federal Deposit Insurance Corporation, and the mindless routines of the large industrial organizations and the military. The social forms of Consciousness II are the committee and the project. Its financial mode is the government grant and the cost-plus contract. The trade unions are fine examples of this form of thought, as is Russian Communism.

I think Reich has made some improvements on my earlier analysis of the American population into an old mentality and a new mentality. I believe his division of the older mentality into Consciousness I and II is sound. But I do not believe that he has adequately treated Consciousness III, or the new mentality. For example, Reich has no place in Consciousness III for the political activist, and I am sure that the activistic student belongs to the newer form of consciousness. I do not believe that the activist is in the same case as the hippie, however. I would divide the new mentality into two parts, A and B. Consciousness III-A is the psychological state of the politically motivated youth in the film *Prologue*. It is heavy with some of the same emphasis as Consciousness I and II, for example, in its reliance on effort and violence. Consciousness III-B, however, is that of the true hippie, and is represented in *Prologue* by the blond boy with the guitar. This state of being has given up all violence and all caring for "success" as measured in the older terms. The blond boy wants only to play his music and find a peaceful place for himself. In a very real sense, Consciousness III-B is utterly new, whereas III-A is but a bridge between Consciousness II and III. Perhaps the organization man and the political activist may be able to make peace with each other, whereas neither I, II, nor III-A will ever be able to understand and tolerate Consciousness III-B.

Let us return to the analogy of the Andean Indian and the hippie, as well as to the theme of the taboo.

In the old adventure films we recall that the taboo was represented by the ugly Oriental idol with a beautiful ruby eye. The American was tempted to steal the jewel, yet was frightened by the magic of the idol—and by the ten thousand headhunters who worshiped it. The hippie is something like that. We are attracted by the gentleness and sensibility of some hippie ways, but frightened by other aspects of his lifestyle.

Rudolf Otto, in *The Idea of the Holy*,[22] tells us that the sacred (and hence, the taboo) is characterized by its *awesomeness* (its terrifying quality) and by its *fascination* (its attractive power). We are both drawn to and repelled by the holy—or the taboo. It is funny, perhaps, or else very perceptive, that many hippie leaders are called "holy men."

For Consciousness II it is utterly important that one take a job with General Motors, for then if he should break his neck, he is covered by insurance, and in twenty years, in any event, he can retire. It is a myth of satisfactory service and the deferral of pleasure just as in Consciousness I. If one is good and does what the boss tells him to do, he can go to Florida for two weeks and "let it all hang out." One can even take his secretary out if he isn't caught by his immediate supervisor. It is the myth of Consciousness II that is the direct adversary of Consciousness III.

In the terms of existentialism we must say that the forms of coming to grips with life seen in Consciousness I and II are examples of bad faith.

The Toilet Myth and the Myth of Space

Consciousness I and II are basically composed of two myths, the toilet myth and the open-space myth. The hippies have overcome the toilet myth but not the open-space myth. Daniel Boone illustrates the Consciousness I myth of open space, and the suburbs illustrate the myth of open space for Consciousness II. The toilet myth is explained by Philip Slater, chairman of the sociology department at Brandeis University, in his brilliant book *The Pursuit of Loneliness*.[23] Briefly, by his title phrase, Slater means that the American who shares the older forms of consciousness believes "out of sight, out of mind."

The toilet myth explains why such a heavy emphasis

is placed upon disposable products in America. If something is used or dirty or offends us, we want to throw it away, flush it away, imprison it out of sight, bury it. The heavy emphasis upon doing away with the garbage is responsible for our pouring our sewage into the nearest river. If it is carried five miles away, we are content; we do not think about what it does to the river and other people. If people of another race move into our neighborhood, or if city conditions become hard for us, we want to shut out the bad conditions by living in locked apartment buildings and trying to keep the people of other colors penned up in ghetto areas. If the other people won't stand still for this, then we want to put them in jail, where they are hidden from our sight. Ultimately, if they persist in making their problematic existence visible, we are tempted to kill them by the use of the police or the National Guard. The same outlook is true concerning college students: we want them to stay on their campuses and out of sight.

We have a whole rationale of forgetting the unpleasant things we do not want to face. We dress up a dead body and paint it so that it looks better than it did when it was alive. We try to hide sexuality by paint and powder and padded clothes. When we drink water, we want to throw away the paper cup, for we have the absurd feeling that our germs are different from the germs in the mouth of someone else. The popularity of paper plates and even paper clothes, along with the planned obsolescence of cars and refrigerators and stereo sets, is all part of the toilet myth.

In this way we cut ourselves off from building up any tradition. Once a pair of shoes has been worn enough to be comfortable, we throw them away and get new ones. Once we have snugly settled down in our house, we want a bigger one. Once a building has grown old enough to have interest and style, we want to tear it down and put up a glass skyscraper. We are very much like the fabulous snake in the fairy tale that is busy eating its own tail. Because of this drive, we cannot develop a sense of history.

The toilet myth leads on naturally into the myth of open space, for when the people we do not like become too numerous, too pent up, we flush ourselves away and move to the country. When the pile of beer cans becomes too high for comfort, we move to a new homestead. The joke that says we must change cars because the ashtray is full is not quite a joke. We are the descendants of generations of people who have become proud of the heritage of moving away from every problem. Unfortunately we ran into the Pacific Ocean long ago, and moving west no longer solves our problems. To some degree the hippie is as much a victim of the myth of open space as is the bearer of the old mentality. It is this myth which makes the commune movement so attractive. In the movie *Prologue,* the boy with the blond beard represents the hippie love of open space, whereas the young man selling the radical newspaper represents the realistic person who knows we must go back into the cities and fight to solve our problems.

The Holy Among the Hippies

The ancient Greeks had one word for both angel and devil—*daemon.* The demonic, for them, was both good and evil by turns. The gods gave life and took it, upheld human honor by coming down to fight by men's sides at Troy, and simultaneously dishonored them by seducing their wives and daughters. The holy, for the Greeks, was a taboo, in the sense that the anthropologist and the historian of religion use that term. The holy both repelled and fascinated, inspired disgust and inspired admiration. The holy, like the taboo of the primitive tribe, was awesome and respected, fled from and feared.

Among the Hindus, the *fakir* or holy man, the guru or religious teacher, also partakes somewhat of the taboo. He is admired for his wisdom and devotion, but his physical appearance and weird state of consciousness disgusts and repels the average man.

Think now of Alan Ginsberg, the hippie poet, homosexual, and chanter of mystical phrases. His poetry demands respect even from the academics, and yet it repels most "straight" people because it is replete with four-letter words and references to less than average experiences and practices. On stage, Ginsberg draws crowds because he puts on a good show. Yet he would be closed down in most towns because of his appearance, words, and general attitude. Ginsberg is often called a holy man in the context of the recent interest in the occult. He fits the taboo pattern rather neatly.

It is not only the Greeks for whom the holy, the taboo, contains *both* the heights of the sublime and the uttermost in degradation. Among the ancient Canaanites and Syrians the god Baal was worshiped by the acts of sacred prostitution. Among the Philistines and Phoenicians the gods were even worshiped by male homosexual prostitutes. It was considered the height of piety to give oneself to full sexual exercise with all comers in the temple or at certain holy seasons. Need we mention that human sacrifice, actual sacred murder, was practiced by the people of the Middle East in Old Testament times, and even by the Israelites? Have we forgotten the *herem,* the holy war, in which all conquered people were murdered? Have we forgotten the noble Aztecs of Mexico, who tore the hearts of youths from their bodies with stone knives to honor their god, the sun?

Dostoyevsky made the connection of holiness and the ultimate in what traditional religion called sin, in his novel *Crime and Punishment.*[24] Sonia, the young girl who prostituted herself in order to support her younger brothers and sisters, is knelt to, by Raskolnikov, the student-murderer, and called holy. As Jesus observed, it is the intention of the heart, not the action of the outer man, that marks the difference between good and evil. For Dostoyevsky, as for the New Testament, and for modern existentialism, it is not the appearance of the face or the actions of the man but the kind of light in the eyes and the belief of the heart that marks the boundary of the holy and the demonic.

Who has not been harmed by the righteous? Who has not been helped by the wicked? In the crucible of combat we have learned that the good can come from the most unlikely sources, and the evil from those sworn to uphold justice. The nonbelieving doctor in Albert Camus's book *The Plague*[25] makes common cause with the Catholic priest, for they come to see that both want the good, and neither really believes much more than the other. Langdon Gilkey, a theologian, has told, in his book *Shantung Compound,* of his experience as a prisoner of war of the Japanese. He found that the most trustworthy man in camp was the man of the poorest reputation, a drunkard. Under duress and strain, ministers and businessmen broke down and stole food; only the drunk could be trusted with the rice.

The good and the evil things we meet in this world, as we live our way through it, bear little relation to the traditional and popular notions of the good and the bad. The holy, when we meet it, so often is smeared with mud and cow dung, as in the Indian guru. Or the holy one is crazed with drugs or stupefied with fasting and meditation, as in the case of the Buddhist monk or the New Guinea witch doctor. Whatever other commendable features middle-class Christian morality may have, probably few people would hold that it inspires us as holy.

The disturbing thing about so many of the hippies is that *they do both attract us and repel us.* They fascinate the straight world and at the same time disgust it. This ambivalent attitude on the part of the straight world is clearly brought out in the movie *Joe.* Joe "hates" the hippies, and yet is irresistibly lured by the promise of the good feelings of the drugs and the startlingly sensual sexuality of the hippie "chicks." Of course, the inhibited mind cannot live with that ambivalence, and once Joe "falls" from grace, someone must die—and it is the taboo object, the hippie, who is killed.

In a society of "Joes," where restrictive and limited minds are pandered to, we can probably expect the ritual sacrifice of "hippies" to prove no exception, but an event that repeats itself. The point of *Joe* and *Easy Rider,* though they are thought cheap and shallow by many liberal critics, is clearly seen to be right by the radical critic. The hippie murders in Detroit, allegedly done by a middle-class father, should warn us of the future.

There are two things going on in the movies *Medium Cool* and *Prologue*. One is a radical criticism of straight society and its political system, because both involve the Chicago convention and police riot there. The other thing is the major point of who is "hip" and who is not. The point of both seems to be that the "hip" person is going to be taking a very serious look at this business of protesting against the system or perhaps even engaging in violent conduct toward the government. Yet the point of both seems also to be a very, very ancient one. "All who take the sword will perish by the sword." I think this is brought out very clearly in these two films, in fact redundantly in *Medium Cool;* and it is also implied in *Prologue*. In *Easy Rider* the theme is that he who is so far outside society that he outrages people's sensibility must accept the possibility of being killed by people whose impulses are not curbed by the niceties of a higher education.

Now what does the whole business about Consciousness III-A and III-B mean? We go back to our original analogy that Consciousness III-B is a set of passivity-like traits, like those of the Indians of the Peruvian mountains and the Andean regions. We have to observe that insofar as they are similar to the Indians, the hippies are going nowhere. We then would have to call it a *static* as opposed to a dynamic movement. On the other hand Consciousness III-A, the politically activistic movement, is a *dynamic* form of thought, as it is a dynamic form of life. Now it may be going nowhere too, in the sense that we assume its failure, but at least it is going somewhere in the sense of taking action, and it is multiplying itself. The analogy would probably be to the revolutionaries of history, for example, the American, the French, and the Cuban revolutionaries. The point then becomes very moot as to the degree in which the mentality of the political activists is similar to the mentality of the most conservative form of older thought? What kind of new action really is it?

Very simply stated, the theme of insurrection is not new; in fact, it is as old as history. Almost all forms of consciousness, religions, philosophies, political systems, and so forth ultimately make insurrection and revolution respectable. Most systems that now exist came into being because of an insurrection or revolution. To that degree, to propose violent action is not really to go outside the given system. It doesn't matter whether you live in the United States, Russia, Cuba, or Canada, *one is really operating within the old system if he proposes to commit insurrection,* because the use of force and violence is part of that old system. To the degree that younger people and their older allies are suggesting that man has to rise to the occasion of a revolutionary jump in consciousness, it would seem that any appeal to violence would make a new shift of consciousness inapplicable.

I think this is also what troubles most people today. What kind of alternative are we proposing when we propose that we are tired of the violence of older systems, whether it be by Marxists, capitalists, or what have you, *if we propose violence* in its place? How refreshing, startlingly new and different can it possibly be? This has two immediate consequences, speaking only politically and scientifically. The first is that it paralyzes the possibility of revolution. I think we are living in that period right now. People are not sure, and from my own point of view, probably *quite rightly not sure*. Because it really doesn't matter who is on top if he's a bastard, a real life-hater, who doesn't love life and people. Is it really worth the effort to change masters, if the new ones are the same kind of masters as the present ones? The Harvard rebellion had a sign that said, "A revolution without joy is hardly worth the trouble." This is profoundly true.

The first consequence of this insight is the onset of paralysis of the possibility of revolution. We are not likely to have a country-wide revolution in this country because of this ambiguity in everyone's mind, which may be one of the saving graces in our history. Secondly, however, it makes *the option of utter passivity*, dropping out, or "copping out," more attractive to the Western mind than it would otherwise be. It is uncharacteristic of Americans to accept passivity, and meditation, and copping out. Every one of us has had ground into us the doctrine that we ought to work like mad, get all we can, run all we can, do all we can, be as visible and active as we can in the world. *To suddenly reverse all that is freaky*, to say the least. It would not be so attractive if there were not this ambivalence like a roadblock at the point of dynamic action. This makes it much more attractive than it would be otherwise.

What Can We Conclude?

We are living through a transitional period in lifestyles that is as radical and dislocative as any such period of change since the Renaissance. Now, as in the birth period of the New World in the West, there is a widespread, soul-deep disillusionment with the styles of life men inherited from the past. Now, as then, there are a multitude of experiments by the alienated and creative people in our culture. Some of these new life-styles are only mild rejections of middle-class culture, others are radical, even revolutionary. Many of the new life-styles conflict with each other as much as they do with the older forms of responding to the world. Some new life-styles will surely prove ephemeral. But what is not ephemeral is the real need to create new forms of life to express and support the new insights into what it means to be a man that have been achieved by the creative and sensitive members of Western civilization over the past few decades.

Chapter 5

RELIGION
IN AN AQUARIAN MODE

How many devout mouths have cried out, "Revive us again!" But how many devout hearts have believed such a revival of Christian religion to be possible at this time, in this place? And how many devout eyes are capable of seeing the movement of the Spirit as it brings such a revival in the modes and the moods of real men and women in the late twentieth century?

The answers to these questions are: (1) millions; (2) not a great number; and (3) only a few, if any of us.

Yet religion *is* undergoing revival, not in just a generally religious, but in a specifically Christian modality in the early 1970's. The signs are writ large so that he who runs by them in his speeding car can read them *if he knows the language of need, despair, faith, hope, love, and salvation.* A vacuum pulls everything loose into itself, and a spiritual vacuum has developed in American culture. First to fly into this vacuum of the human heart was the occasional, loosely settled Oriental teacher or Buddhist bonze. Next came the more traditional Hindu evangelistic sects, already long at work in Europe and America. Then, the outer fringes of the temple of occultism, theosophy, anthroposophy,

Divine Science. And then, the full range of occultism, from astrology to palmistry to dream interpretation to witchcraft, in its white and black forms. Can we wonder that this material has not plugged the gap, the hole in the middle of things for millions of modern American youth?

Is it a surprise that the vacuum has now pulled into itself that figure which has been given the least attention by the organized church—the vision of the man Jesus of Nazareth? Are we so socially insensitive that we cannot see that only a religious element that is part and parcel of Western cultural experience can possibly meet the needs of the members of Western countries? Even the semi-Marxist Latin revolutionaries look to the figure of Jesus carrying a rifle, or to his face on a "Wanted" poster. (Both of these images of Jesus are widely accepted among American young people.) *Jesus Christ Superstar* [1] was destined to come—and it is here.

Jesus Christ—Youth Folk-Hero

I remember vividly my seminary days in the South some sixteen years ago. One of my fellow seminarians, from South Carolina, had a little "sacred place" on his study desk. It resembled an icon in an Orthodox home, or a statue of the Virgin in a Catholic household. This young man's icon was, however, a photograph of General Robert E. Lee, flanked by miniature Confederate flags.

Recently I was a visitor to two seminaries, both in the free-church Protestant tradition. Neither was "liberal" in the old meaning of the word, nor overly conservative. Prominently displayed in many of the students' rooms was the record album *Jesus Christ Super-*

star, as well as various depictions of the Christ as a hippie, an outcast, or a revolutionary. If this "new" view of Jesus were limited to seminarians, it would not be as important a phenomenon as it actually is. However, a fascination with Jesus Christ is common to thousands of college and high school students across the United States. I have had only to mention, for example, the record *Superstar* to have numbers of students come to my classrooms or office with their own copies, wanting me to listen to it with them. I have seen the newly founded "free university" of a large regional state university offer as one of its first four courses a class on "Jesus and the Jesus Freaks."[2] I have been moved by some of this new-found attraction to the figure of Jesus, more emotionally touched than I can recall being since a Jewish girl years ago showed me her copy of *Barabbas* by Pär Lagerkvist[3] saying, "My husband and I have become fascinated by Jesus."

What is it that attracts so many youth today to Jesus Christ at least as a culture hero, an exemplary historical character, if not as something "more"? What is it that is contained in his character, as interpreted by a number of creative, modern people, that is able to outweigh the "turn off" on Jesus that many young people received from their churches? Jesus must come through on some deep, symbolic level to be able to escape from the "plastic," pious frame put around him by the average church school leader. Actually, the character of Christ does carry this symbolic power, as well as exhibiting in his life story the same kinds of doubts, anxieties, and crises that contemporary young people find themselves passing through. The record album *Jesus Christ Super-*

star makes obvious the connection of Jesus' identity crisis and the identity crisis of late adolescence today. The Jesus of the rock opera, like many young men today, is not quite clear about who he is or what he should do. He has idealistic convictions and vague ideas about how they should be implemented, but he is far from sure. As in the Gospel record, the Jesus of the opera becomes more anxious and agitated as *the directions in which he must move become clear.* In words of great beauty and psychological power, the lyricist [4] presents the doubts and fears of a young man who is horrified to face the fact that he must die, now. Jesus faces ultimate anxiety in an ultimate situation.

The Mood of Ultimacy

Like it or not, many young persons have a sense of ultimacy about our current social and historical situation, a sense that might fairly be called "eschatological" in the Biblical sense. There is a mood of ultimacy, a mood of eschatological anxiety abroad in the land. Nowhere is this mood seen more surely than in the environmental conservation movement. The professors, scientists, students, and nature lovers of every profession who man our Earth Day platforms and who picket industrial polluters have a very real and present eschatological sense. In plain speech, they visualize "the end of the world," the end not only of human life but of all life, if we do not cease poisoning the land, air, and water and reverse our present activities. This background awareness that we may be stifling the roots of life itself with our own garbage sets the mood for the life-style of many today. The name of this mood is "ultimate anxiety," focused on the end of life itself as a continuing possibility.

The Martyred Young Man

The image of the crucified idealist, Jesus Christ, became very real for those who were at all close to the civil rights struggle. It is not hard for men and women who were at Selma or at Orangeburg, South Carolina, to visualize Jesus Christ as black and as killed by police bullets. It is not difficult for committed Christians such as Charles Ashanin, a white professor then at Orangeburg, to understand the nightmares suffered by his Lord, who was a "true man." How can those of us who at last timidly stood up to be counted as Christ's disciples think of Martin Luther King, Jr., and not think of Christ? How can those of us who deplored the escalation of the Indochina war from the very beginning, such as Robert McAfee Brown and Thomas J. J. Altizer, not respond in spirit to the now-famous cover of *Ramparts* magazine which shows Jesus Christ crucified between two American soldiers?

Our anxiety had, by 1964, become commitment, and our commitment, by 1968, with the murder of King and Kennedy and the shooting of the Orangeburg students, had become outrage. Kent State and Jackson State in 1970 only spread the sense of outrage to others. For those who knew Orangeburg and Selma, the horror and antagonism were already there. We saw the world—and we see it still—under the rubric and through the lens of the crucified Christ whose disciples are also persecuted.

RELIGION IN AN AQUARIAN MODE 131

It was only a matter of time until this mood of Calvary, of ultimacy, would be shared by our students. Part of the rise of the "new mentality" was always the growing sense of awareness that the champions of life and goodness—Christ and Gandhi, King and the Kennedys—were always persecuted. In some this insight induced the outrage that led to political radicalism; in others it forced a turn toward quietism: these we called "hippies."

The Hippie Christ

Way back in the "beat" generation of the 1950's, the poet Lawrence Ferlinghetti zeroed in on the figure of the crucified Christ as a symbol of the times. The poem caused quite a stir at the time, raising the hairs of the pious and the interest of the young. I remember a freshman student bringing me a copy of Ferlinghetti's "Christ Climbed Down . . ." in 1959.[5] It was an image of Jesus he could understand, a picture of a real person sickened by the plastic inauthenticity of the modern Christmas tree, who "climbed down" from the tinseled tree and "ran away." It was to be a span of less than five years from the creation of this portrait of an honest human being, shunning the sham of pietism and commercialism combined, to the emergence of the wall posters showing Jesus to be what he actually was, a "wanted man," a Socrates condemned for treason and blasphemy, a revolutionary.

In this same period the work of Father Groppi in Milwaukee was going on, symbolized by the picture of a black man rising up, breaking the chains of prejudice and discrimination, with the motto, "Hallelujah, He Is

Risen" emblazoned underneath.

Perhaps for the first time since Francis of Assisi came ministering to the dying plague victims, Jesus Christ was restored to his rightful place as the symbol of the love of God for, and the hope of man in, the underdog. The power to resist oppression, the power to release deep wells of the courage that was latent in the Christ symbol, was let loose. Even for the radical theologian who announced the death of God, the "man who was for others" was alive and well, and with his people again.

The person who was radically religious and/or oriented toward social-problems lost, in many cases, his position in the church or other institution, or at least lost much financial support, but he won one thing—the victory of radical religion. He won back the symbol and figure of Christ for the cause of human justice.[6]

Now Jesus Christ no longer "belongs" to the church as an institution (he really never did), but to our secular culture. He "belongs to" those who "belong to" him, the latent church of believers and doubters and unbelievers who have entered the unequal struggle to make human life possible and human again in the face of institutionalized selfishness and violence, public and private, North and South, at home and abroad, capitalist and communist, white and black.

Now, in their thousands, more young people are coming forward to help carry his cross. Not on our lapels or over our robes, but in the streets and into jail. The present and the coming kingdom can be seen, flowing in from all directions, in the Berrigans and the Groppis, in the Jesus Freaks and the new styles of ministry of thousands of young clergymen and laymen.

If War Is Peace, Peace May Well Be War

For millions of the radicalized, there appears to be a hidden agenda for the Vietnam War: the diversion of public attention from domestic social problems. The attention span of so many citizens is so short, and their capacity for open-mindedness is so limited, that such a benefit from an overseas war is easily achieved by leaders cynical enough to adopt such a policy. But whatever is hidden sooner or later comes to light. And the light has slowly grown in intensity since 1967, so that now most Americans can at least see dimly the outlines of our present social position. Despite the election of the more conservative party in 1968, public support for the Indochina war has steadily declined from the frenzy stirred up by the pseudo events in the Tonkin Gulf in 1964. Yet the events of the Nixon administration, pledged to "wind down" the war, have (despite large troop withdrawals) served to widen the war to Cambodia and Laos and to intensify the problem of a peace settlement. The end of an American involvement in Indochina is nowhere in sight. However, the Christian must ask the question, "What will happen when the war is over?"

The Price of Our Salvation

The price of the old man's salvation, the cost of being born again, of moving from Consciousness I and II to the new mentality of Consciousness III, may well be more suffering. Revolutionary men and women are springing up everywhere, but only as individuals, or couples, or little groups in suburbs, on farms, or in college dorms or student housing areas. But while there is this slight marginal gain in the growth of bearers of the new mentality, there appears to be a mass movement toward conservatism (Consciousness I) burgeoning in America. As I have discussed the political and social reasons for this conservative reaction in an earlier book,[7] I will not go into details on that phenomenon here. Let us confine ourselves to the religious and moral aspects of this paradoxical development of progressive consciousness (even *radical* consciousness) among the few, along with a reactionary, culture-lag-type movement among the many. What is happening is a widening of the consciousness gap and a consequent exaggeration of the generation gap.

Let us now turn to examine in some detail what we noted briefly in another connection earlier in this book. A youthful movement toward traditional religion has elicited wide notice and comment in the early 1970's. This is "the Jesus movement," sometimes called "the Jesus People" or even "the Jesus Freaks."

Jesus Freaks—Fundamentalism Reborn? [8]

The Jesus Freaks, a growing part of the American youth scene, can be best described as a subculture within a subculture. They make up a movement that is sweeping the nation with the ideas of brotherly love, unity, peace, fellowship, and a fundamentalist view of the teachings of Christ.

The beginning of the movement is vague. It would be extremely difficult, if not impossible, to pinpoint the birth of the new wave at an exact time and location, but it came out of the youth culture which freaked out, tuned in and turned on to drugs, promiscuous sex, communal living, and a new way of life destined to break the already tight situation between the generations. This youth subculture threw away the ideals of capitalism and most other political ideologies, striving to find a better life than the one that they were told they were destined to live. Though there were many problems in the "counter culture," it flourished for a long while as the only escape from what the establishment termed "the good life": the treadmill of college, a job from nine to five, a home in the suburbs, two children, a wife, a variety of credit cards, and assorted bills. The new subculture attempted to give life itself more meaning, and in this striving made several attempts at forming utopian societies. Its downfall was the misuse of harmful drugs and the disintegration of its original ideal of a better society, a disintegration speeded by the impact of sensuality and the selfish pursuit of inner pleasure.

Out of this "hip" counter culture came a second subculture, people who had weeded out the parts of the first subculture that they felt did not function adequately and who had revamped its ideas. Finally, after making the circuit of ideas to model, from the Eastern forms of mysticism to the formality of the present church, some young people determined to live the kind of life pictured in the Bible, especially imitating the life of Christ. This new group, already named (by other youth) the "Jesus Freaks," is now moving over the nation proclaiming a new life dedicated to the good of man and the praise of Jesus Christ. Though this movement has many aspects and many different factions, its members all have the same creed: that Jesus Christ is the Son of God, sent to deliver men from hell, if only men accept his way. Because of this stress on the New Testament picture of Jesus, they have come to an absolutely literal interpretation of the Bible. In their opinion, anyone who does not live by the Bible is damned.

Hundreds of "Jesus People" churches, centers, and communes have opened in the past year and a half in storefronts and old houses all over California. Their "Bible raps," "Jesus teach-ins," and "Jesus rock concerts" are listed in the back of the *Hollywood Free Paper,* just as personal sex ads are listed in *The Los Angeles Free Press,* says Duane Pederson, the editor. Pederson admits he modeled his Jesus paper after the Los Angeles underground weekly.

The sudden blossoming of the Jesus People clearly caught establishment churches and religious scholars by surprise. Some of them still don't know how to react. Robert S. Ellwood, a professor of religion at the University of Southern California, says that until recently it appeared that religion among the young was moving toward mysticism, expansion of consciousness and Eastern beliefs. But drugs and meditation didn't deliver what they promised. Consequently, says Mr. Ellwood, many young people are rejecting the configuration of symbols and gods in the "head mysticism" of the 1960's and are focusing on one man—Jesus. They feel they are reaching the same kind of infinity consciousness—but without drugs or meditation.[9]

The Jesus Freaks have separated themselves from the established church, since they don't feel that the religion of the older generation relates to them. The church was not even aware of the new movement until it was well under way and had power in itself. An official of the National Council of Churches in New York says, "Campus ministers have been telling us, 'Man, something is happening, but we're not quite sure what it is.'" Another official of the NCC expresses a common uncertainty among churchmen when he says, "We know there's a widespread, grass roots, evangelical nonchurch somewhere out there that's reaching a lot of young people." [10]

A large segment of the Jesus Freak movement is led by an ordained Baptist minister, twenty-nine-year-old Arthur Blessitt. Blessitt dresses and acts much as any other person in the "hip" culture, yet he preaches and witnesses in bars, massage parlors, "head shops," and rock music clubs. He runs a house on Sunset Strip called "His Place," where he trys to bring the Word of God to the people of the "hip" culture: pushers, teenagers from the suburbs, dopers, and motorcyclists. When Blessitt was asked what this revolution of youth consisted of, his reply was: "The revolution going on here is the very same revolution that Jesus Christ has been bringing about in the hearts of men since his life on earth. It's a revolution of love, because God is love, and he can be known personally through Christ. Jesus was in the life-changing business long ago; he died to pay the penalty of our sin and selfishness, and rose again—he can live in our hearts today and change us completely!" [11]

In an article for *Look,* Brian Vachon characterized the Jesus Freak movement in the following manner: "A crusade—a massive, fundamentalist, Christ-as-personal-Savior revival—has caught hold in California, and it shows every sign of sweeping East and becoming a national preoccupation. It's an old time, Bible-toting, witness-giving kind of revival, and the new evangelists are the young. They give their Christian message with cheerful dedication: Turn on to Jesus. He's coming. Soon." [12]

This is the feeling of many persons taking part in the movement. They are preparing the world for the second coming of Christ, which they feel is imminent. Using Biblical quotations, they predict the end of the world in a very short time. The "Children of God," a segment of the Jesus movement, have put out a tract entitled "Are We Living in 'THE TIME OF THE END?'" In this tract they predict the events to come and the time when the end of the world will arrive. All this is done by using Biblical quotations. One tract observes:

> The Bible has many prophecies concerning the fate of nations. In 600 B.C. Jeremiah prophesied that the broad walls of Babylon would be broken (51.58) and that *none* of the great stones would ever be used again (51.26). The city was destroyed beginning in 535 B.C. Since then, cities have been built near the site of Babylon. But they have not used those expensive stones that were quarried at great cost. The wall was 60 miles long, 200 feet high and 90 feet wide. Why have those useful stones remained untouched for 2500 years? GOD!! [13]

The "Children of God" is a wandering religious tribe led by Arnold (Joshua) Dietrich, age twenty-nine. The tribe began two and a half years ago in Dietrich's native New York City. Picking up converts, he traveled the country, preaching from the Bible from a fast-growing caravan of cars and buses. The tribe found a home at a rescue mission in August, 1970. The mission's owner, Rev. Fred Jordan, allowed the tribe to set up a training headquarters on his four-hundred-acre ranch near Thurber, Texas.

The Children of God are now spreading across the United States by a method called "colonization." They send out twenty or thirty people to live in a new town every time someone in that area tells them they may live there in a house or on a farm. When people enter the tribe, they give up all their worldly possessions to the group. To make the movement grow, these possessions are redistributed to those who need them. All this colonization is controlled from their headquarters in Texas, which they have named the "Texas Soul Clinic." From this headquarters they decide who is to go to live at the new colony.

Everyone who joins their group has to go to Texas for an intensive study and growth process. There they receive training in the Bible and in different methods of witnessing. After they are sent out to a colony, they continue to study the Bible four to six hours a day, spending the rest of their time on the street witnessing. By this witnessing they make more converts and with the converts comes all their property. So the movement continues to grow.

The *Abilene Reporter* carried a story about the "Children of God" written by James Dublin. In it Dublin tells what the Children think about themselves:

One person who reads this might consider himself very religious. Another may think himself "groovy" to satisfy his religious yearnings with highs on pot, speed or acid.

But no matter what his convictions, any person from any group could make a trip to a little settlement called the "Children of God" commune and learn more about himself and his beliefs in one afternoon than he could ever imagine.

The commune is easy to find: Just take a trip to Thurber, 16 miles east of Ranger, and ask the attendant at the Thurber service station how to get there.

Very simply, the settlement is made up of about 175 young people, average age 20, who have tired of hypocrisy, materialism and hate (Mankind has an unfortunate abundance of all three qualities) and have retreated from it to find something else.

However, this is not one of the run-of-the-mill "tune in, turn on, drop out" hippie communes. This group has no intentions of running away from the world. Instead, they intend to change it—for the better.

They attend classes five to six hours a day in individual study. And another three hours in manual labor for the cause.

All this is in preparation for re-entering the everyday world and converting more followers. What's the cause?

The cause, says spiritual leader, Jonathan Hosea Levi, is Jesus Christ.

"There is no drug use, smoking, drinking or free love here," he said, "only God."

"We try to live as was written in the Biblical book of Acts," the 21-year-old Levi said. *"It's not what we believe in that strikes people but the way we live. We're an example proving that it's possible to live just like the Apostles did."*

"Most people are afraid to just pull up, quit their jobs and join a group like this, but we have proven that if everyone pools their resources and pulls together then it's all possible. The only way to learn about God and serve Him is to live with Him," he said.[14]

Another segment of this movement is the *Hollywood Free Paper*, a religious underground paper attempting to spread the Word and keep all the factions of the movement aware of what everyone else is doing. Published in a number of cities, it claims a circulation of 260,000, and bulk copies of the paper are shipped to all fifty states as well as to eleven countries. The *Hollywood Free Paper* claims to be the largest underground paper in the world. It runs stories of what is happening and what world events are taking place and how these events correlate with the movement's view of the Bible. In the back of the paper are run what look like ads, but is news of where religious events will take place and all the information one would need to attend these events.[15]

Upon examination of this movement, we see it as possessing the potential power to reach around the world. The problems that appear in the movement are the lack of ability to relate genuinely to the present world and to aid in working through social problems. Jesus Freaks live by their vision of the Bible completely. They differ from the extremely fundamentalist religious groups already in existence only in that they maintain that these religions only live the Bible on Sunday and they are living it every day.

We must observe that the Jesus Freaks cover so small an area of human problems in their thought that it is doubtful that the movement will last. Its only hope for survival is to colonize to such an extent that it will, in essence, have created its own world, not dependent on or relating to the present culture, except as a place to go to attempt to get converts.

One of my students, Jim Blair, of Louisville, Kentucky, assessed the Jesus People rather negatively, Blair reported:

> After talking with these people, I was struck with the fact that they do not think for themselves, they only imitate what they are told to do. I did not feel that the majority had really given any individual thought to who God is or what it means to give your life to Him. I felt that they were simply jumping on a band wagon that was going their way, and when the wagon failed to provide what they wanted they would jump off just as fast as they had jumped on. In general I felt that very few of them could stand alone (with God) before mankind and really make any impression with their religion. They lacked personal commitment to God, and were trying to substitute a commitment to man (their leaders) in its place. Instead of actually living for God as individuals they were living in a group of people who professed certain beliefs. As long as it was possible they were going to stay with that group, since it was comfortable and provided a crusade to live through, a battle to fight where no one could be injured. In general, the movement is a place to hide from reality. Instead of trying to work through the problems of the world, "Jesus Freaks" have labeled these problems the "will of God." By doing this they turn their backs on the world to live in their own idealistic world of unreality.[16]

I might add that the Jesus People talk a good ball game, but are, so far, pretty poor hitters in the fields of race relations, poverty, and the struggle against war.

Summing Up Religion Today

For all the predictions that religion is dead or dying, nothing like that seems to be the case. Religion, as an institution, is as large and wealthy and powerful in America today as it was ten or twenty years ago. Compared to the periods of fifty or a hundred years ago, institutional religion is very powerful, indeed. But the impetus toward expansion in terms of numbers and in the building of new congregations *has* been blunted. While there is much money in the church's treasury, it is not coming in as steadily now as it was a few years ago. Perhaps Tillich's idea of the "latent church," of the church-in-the-world outside the boundaries of organized religion, has caught on.

Church membership tends to show a slight decline, but it is not a serious situation as yet. More serious is the financial pinch of church agencies and boards, a pinch produced by the same factors that have slowed the forward progress of higher education, the fiscal policies of the Federal Government. The church, like the university, now suffers from our recession economy.

Religion, in the spiritual sense, is booming. Ours is a period of great interest in the content and promises of every religious tradition. We live in a "spiritual supermarket" in North America. There are multitudes of sects and churches and spiritual philosophies held out to us on every hand. There is no recession in this spiritual market. People, especially young people, are buying. However, they are not always aware that a buyer should beware of the motive of the seller—as well as of the quality of the merchandise.

I am happy over the resurrection of the figure of Jesus at the beginning of the 1970's. The success of *Jesus Christ Superstar* encourages me. I was pleased to see the "Jesus Freaks" arise to counter the "Satan Freaks" and drug freaks of Southern California. But it remains to be seen how truly these new followers of Jesus understand his loving, accepting person. It is not clear that the Jesus People will connect their fundamentalism with the social involvement that was a significant part of Jesus' life. If the nineteenth-century type of spiritual-experience theology that has set free the energies of the Jesus People *can* be joined to the social awareness and courage of the liberal Christian movment, we may be in for a true Christian revival. But if the Jesus movement concentrates on "soul-saving" and flees farther away from our disturbed society, then the future of religion—and of America—is seriously in doubt.

It is in the marketplace, the law court, the factory, and on the parade ground that Jesus must be proclaimed to be Lord, not in the monastery or on a Texas ranch.

Chapter 6

THE PRESENT REVOLUTION—
A DANGEROUS OPPORTUNITY

One young lady, after wrestling with the problem of becoming human in our time, made these observations:

> A few years ago I was deeply interested and concerned with the hippie movement. I read every article I could find in hopes of better understanding the ideas and the way of life they proposed. The concept of brotherhood, world love, a total sharing, a knowing of the self, all appeared appealing. Drugs themselves were extremely fascinating and I wished I could experience their mystifying effects.[1]

The hippie movement is now over. Perhaps this is best, because where there once existed so much plasticity and fakeness, now only the hard core remains. It was as if the people involved saw the movement only as a game, a dream world, like Alice's escape into fantasy. While at first the fantasy was fun and exciting, the pleasure soon wore away as the realities of hunger, cold, and abuse crept in. Instead of being a pleasant trip, it turned into a bad trip for many. Their beliefs were not truly founded in their actions; thus they were not able to rise above physical discomforts. Soon they returned to the corruptness of the established society for comfort. Only a hard core remains. The ideas that emerged are not forgotten; instead, a stronger foundation is laid upon which the future may be built. Those acts which appeared superficial now cease to be. It no longer matters that you have the appearance or that you play the role, dressing oddly and speaking in certain idioms. That false mask drops as the people awaken to the injustices and the discrepancies between the truths held by our society and those actualized in reality. Today many youth seem more sensitive to the world around them and to the needs of others. The concept of brotherhood for such people is more than words. Evidence of this is shown through youthful expressions in demonstrations, marches, peace corps organizations, community centers, Earth Day and clean-up programs.

It is only when we unite in brotherhood, identifying ourselves with others and their situations, that we care and find meaning in life. Many young people realize this today. The true hippie expressed this insight and still does express it in his rebellion against the indifference of established society. A community may arrange it so that a Negro can't get a position as a teacher. Straight people will say: What can you expect? He is a Negro; he doesn't deserve a job. He isn't like us—his skin is black. But the hippie, or hip young person, would retort: He is a man—he is like me.

Another life-style of some young people today seems to be that of escapism. Escape from the problems of society. Escape from involvement with others, escape from themselves. Escape from the challenges crying through the streets, ghettos, rice paddies, suburbs, and cities.

A DANGEROUS OPPORTUNITY

There are several means of escape. One can escape through drugs, alcohol, sex, automobiles, motorcycles, music, movies, and television. One can also escape by simply closing one's eyes and ears to the needs of others. Our student observer remarks:

This is the silent majority's fate! And they must pay dearly for their silence as they accept the injustices and chains imposed upon them. They accept the indifference, the categorizing, the loneliness, the absurdity of life in America. They refuse to be sensitive to the situations confronting them. They refuse to be, but live in nothingness.[2]

At least those who do not speak now still have the time to awaken and speak out if they continue to think in their silence. But how lost are those who do not think at all, denying their humanity and individuality! This is what drug users and alcohol abusers do. They kill their senses and their rationality so that they cannot be confronted by anything except where and how to get their supply to ease their minds. This is death of self, the escape from the attempt to become a man.

A third escape is into fantasy. If a person doesn't like his situation, he will create his own world in which he can think, act, say, and do all that he wishes to do. Yet how wrong to create a world within oneself! One denies himself, and can never really know himself or others. He ceases to be a productive, dynamic, concerned person, but instead becomes static, withdrawn into himself. Being within oneself in that escapist fashion keeps one from ever finding out who he is. He loses contact with other people and events.

A Dangerous Opportunity

We have lived through a series of revolutions in thought in this century, the cumulative impact of which has shaken the foundations of man's very conception of himself as a part of the universe. This shaking of the foundations has destroyed, for millions, the old standards of civil righteousness and religious salvation. That which we once took as self-evident: the primacy of man in the earthly order, the existence of some independence and dignity for any human purpose, the possibility of some real (if limited) areas of freedom for the human creature, all have been challenged by historical events and technological-social changes. In response to this psychic demolition work, the various alternative life-styles studied here have reasserted the meaningfulness of human life in many, often conflicting, ways. Let us now try to analyze the essential forms and meanings of these various new alternative visions of man as they represent revolts against the three traditional conceptions of man.

New Life-Styles Equal New Images of Man

The marks of the new mentality and the new men it is producing are many and varied. Historically, they have arisen out of the social and psychological chaos of the latter half of the twentieth century. The factors and events that have brought about these social, physical, and psychic dislocations are many, and have been discussed at some depth in my earlier works, especially in *The Roots of the Radical Theology* [3] and *The New Mentality*,[4] so I will not try to reestablish them here.

Additionally, the intellectual turmoil of our era has been thoroughly studied by historians, sociologists, psychologists, economists, and political scientists.[5] It has also been investigated by literary scholars such as Marshall McLuhan,[6] and theologians such as Paul Tillich, Reinhold Niebuhr, and H. Richard Niebuhr.[7] The reader is referred to the selected reading list in the Notes for an introduction to what may be called "the mess we have made of man." Another area of information directly bearing on the need for alternative life-styles is the growing number of books, television programs, and magazine articles on the environmental crisis.[8]

The marks of the new mentality or the modes by which youth, and increasing numbers of older adults, are searching for a new vision of what man ought to be, are given exterior expression in the commonly accepted life-styles that now seem to dominate "everyday" fashions in America. These exterior expressions include wearing the hair longer (on both men and women), wearing sideburns or beards and/or moustaches, beads, pins, buttons, patches, bell-bottoms, sandals; going barefoot, hitchhiking, and smoking marijuana. To be sure, these activities and styles are also followed by many people who are essentially "straight" (or old-fashioned), and some bearers of the new mentality don't show their inner orientation by their outer appearance. *The quest for a new image of man, for an alternative life-style is, at base, a changed way of looking at oneself and at the world. It is a shift in consciousness, or, in the terms of the psychiatrist, in the self-process.*[9]

John Cage has written: "Our minds are changing

... from an unrealistic concern with a nonexistent status quo to a courageous seeing things in movement, life as revolution. History is one revolution after another." [10]

Among the marks of the new mentality that are clearer guides than the exterior life-style alone are:

> An emphasis upon discovery of the essential core of one's self, and a development of as many of the potentialities of the individual as is humanly possible.
>
> A rejection of the restrictions of traditional religion and morality in favor of a more flexible code of behavior that bears at least a "family resemblance" to "the new mentality" or "situational ethics." Nothing is taken as right or wrong in and of itself as an act, but is judged only by reference to the persons involved and the situations of their involvement.
>
> An adventurous spirit willing to experiment and take risks. This underlies the "thumb tripping," [11] or co-ed hitchhiking, and the willingness to experiment with drugs and unusual sexual activities.
>
> A thirst to be a whole person, physically as well as mentally and spiritually. This has given birth to the whole Human Potentialities movement, the Esalen Institute, sensitivity training, and the emphasis upon the study of group processes.
>
> A seeing of the world as the sole (or the solely important) locus of human concern, with a lessening (in all but those who are drawn to the mysteries of the occult) of interest in an afterlife with rewards and punishments for the deeds done within history.

A DANGEROUS OPPORTUNITY

Even the rebirth of interest in mysticism has done little to change the *this-worldly* (and more or less sensual) accent of the new mentality.[12] This outlook grows out of the belief that man is responsible for the mess he has made of the world and he is responsible for trying to straighten it out.[13]

Many modern youth and older persons have sought to discover within themselves and their friends, out of their own experiences, a more satisfying image of man than that given by the three major concepts that have dominated the West over the last twenty-four hundred years. These inherited images of man are the *classical* (Aristotle: Man is a rational being), the *Christian* (Paul: Man is a combination of the spiritual and the physical), and the *scientific* (Man is a physical-chemical organism). Many younger people have deliberately flaunted these traditional images by breaking the taboos and restrictions on human conduct that were based on these views.

For example, human *rationality* (the classical view) is rejected by millions today in favor of the irrational, the mystical, the occult. The rejection of reason as the *sine qua non* of human-beingness is demonstrated in the continuing appeal of existentialism, of Zen Buddhism, of astrology and other occult practices. A high valuation of the irrational elements of man underlies the appeal of marijuana and drug experimentation.

Community morals and mores (the Christian image) are rejected by millions who still hold to the rational as a definition of man, as well as by those who have embraced the irrational. The discipline of impulse and desire is rejected in favor of a modern hedonism, a sensual enjoyment of all forms of physical and psychological stimulation. One wonders if the bearers of the new mentality are polymorphously perverse or polymorphously versatile? (Probably the latter.) This rejection explains the new ordering of sexual relationships, drug experiences, hitchhiking by girls, nudity, blue movies, as well as books such as *The Sensuous Woman* and *The Sensuous Man*.

The conceptual system of orderliness in nature leading to the development of logical, scientific methods of dealing with the world and with people (the scientific view) is now rejected by many in favor of the romantic, the adventurous, the mysterious, the poetic, even the religious and the mystical. The gravitation of students from the study of the sciences to the study of the humanities (especially world religions) is a result of this feeling.

Behind most of the dissenting social movements in the latter half of the twentieth century stands one basic perception: a recognition of the worth of life itself in all its forms. The rebels and reformers of our time are telling us that before we can have respect for man, we must have respect for life, since man is but one expression of life. The revolutionary activities that led to independence for India and Pakistan, for Algeria, the black African states and Cuba, began out of a basic perception that the life of a man, be he black or white, European or colonial, educated or not, was precious.

The Algerian physician, Frantz Fanon, points out the need of the colonial peasant for an image of man as a moral revolutionary in *The Wretched of the Earth*.[14] Fanon describes how the "second-class" treatment of colonial peoples makes them less than men, and debases the value of all of life for them. He strongly suggests that one can win his sense of humanity, in such a colonial situation, only by killing the oppressor. Studies of oppressed Negroes in the United States also reveal the psychically debilitating effects of having the value of one's life depressed by exploitation and prejudice. It is not strange that Eldridge Cleaver fled to Algeria after fighting to enhance the self-image of the black man and woman in America. Cleaver, and many other young intellectuals of minority groups in the United States, see the problem of making America a truly democratic, pluralistic society precisely in the light of combating the process of dehumanization of those who lack economic and political power in this country. The exploitation of the weak and poor (including the white poor in the South, where some areas do not even *allow* labor unions) [15] in America is, first of all, a robbery of the humanity (the manhood and womanhood) of the classes at the bottom of the power structure.

The robbery of man's humanity is done by other institutions and by other means than economic ones alone. The university also helps to dehumanize man, as do the bureaucracy of the welfare system, the Armed Forces, the police and courts.

While the old populist notion that the redistribution of land and wealth is the major social problem that America needs to face is true, no political party will any longer support this view. It is also true that the church and the school (from kindergarten to graduate university) also demean and rob the humanity of men and women. The cultural lag that plagues us because many churches will not abjure the morality of the Middle Ages, especially in reference to premarital sex, marriage, divorce, abortion, homosexuality, and the respect due the state, is a major way that man's self-process, the creation of his self-image and his vision of man, is blocked or defeated. Since different religious and ideological groups make differing demands upon the person, he is damned by some if he does anything and damned by others if he doesn't. There are also many instances of conservatives and liberals cooperating to destroy the creative person (usually called "a radical"), which makes one wonder what if any difference there is between organized groups. Each institution seems dedicated to the control of human belief and behavior. The documentation of the erosion of political "liberalism" from a creative leftism to a stifling acceptance of the national and international program of the right has been made by Jack Newfield in his *Playboy* article "The Death of Liberalism." [16]

According to Newfield, "during the fifties, liberalism lost its will to fight and accepted the basic economic and foreign-policy assumptions of the right." [17] Today, he continues, the banner of the left must be recovered and offered to the young, "by restoring the old dignity of the populist attack on monopolies and abusive corporations and banks." [18]

Newfield has done the nation a distinct service in his writings, ranging as they do from his perceptive book, *A Prophetic Minority* [19] to his recent *Playboy* article. He has shown us, convincingly, that the so-called liberal in America, once he is part of the government, is "establishment" in mind as well as in lifestyle. Newfield forces us to admit that the leftism of

A DANGEROUS OPPORTUNITY

liberalism is rhetoric without substance. The radical leftist, therefore, brings us to the same vision as the radical rightist, Phyllis Schlafly,[20] that we do not have genuine political choices any more, but only echoes. By similar tokens, we can judge that much of the New Left program (whatever that might be) is also mere rhetoric, or hysterical action at cross-purposes to human and social needs. What comes from such a negative appraisal is simply this: we need a redemption of the left in America. We need a movement profoundly human as well as profoundly intellectual. We need a leftism akin to the populism of the old South and the Midwest, which expresses the human yearnings and desires of real people, not social theoreticians. We need to care for people and their everyday needs and concerns, hopes, dreams, and fears, not develop a program aimed at affecting the gross national product ("Gross," what a profoundly apt name!) or producing more bureaucratic programs. The left needs to arise from its genuinely new roots in the lovingly turned soil of the People's Park, now asphalted over by the organization men of the state.

To be frank, the possibility of redeeming the left is not great. Too many of the persons capable of bringing about such a rebirth are fragmented, tormented visionaries harried to the self-destructive point of armed revolt. Too many of the natural leaders of the "little people" are partial and provincial in their revolutionary consciousness because they happen to be black, Mexican-American (Chicano), or Amerindian. These leaders of ethnic groups are understandable and admirable within their limits, of course. Their extreme interest in the problems of their own people to the exclusion of interest in other kinds of people is understandable, too. Indeed, the partiality of some black leaders is quite justified, considering the peculiar history of discrimination and slavery of the blacks in America. But this partiality is not politically and socially warranted, nor, in the face of the demonic problems of the 1970's, is such a standpoint forgivable. If we do not hang together, we shall assuredly hang separately. That is a historical proverb that should be tatooed on the hand of everyone who shares in the activistic stream of the new mentality.

We must draw the people together, not again, for they have never been together before, but together for the first time. We must begin to preach the notion given musical expression in Bob Dylan's song, "They're Only a Pawn in Their Game." For as long as the Afros and Chicanos and other ethnic groups "hang loose" from the rest of the people and fight only for themselves, we will not start that long but utterly necessary battle to politicize and win the vast ignorant, defeated army of poor whites who are the backbone (potentially) for a populist movement that would have the size to turn this country around. Perhaps the poor white votes for Wallace simply because Wallace represents himself as some kind of real political choice as opposed to the echoes of each other that are the established parties. Who knows what would happen if a leader with the charisma and paradigmatic style of a Huey Long, but with better moral and political insight, were to rise up from the people again?

The natural leaders of the so-called "silent majority" are not foredoomed to be right-wingers. Huey Long,

"Pitchfork Ben" Tilman (of South Carolina), and William Jennings Bryan were conservatives on racial, religious, and (public) moral issues, but politically and personally they were radicals of the left. With the spread of Consciousness III or the new mentality to all sections of the country and among all classes of youth (it has *not* yet reached the lower-class and lower-middle-class white youth), we may witness the rise of many native, populist radicals again. One can only hope that the popularity of Charles Reich, with his penchant for denigrating the need for political involvement, will not instill a new social "quietism" in the developing citizens of tomorrow.

Finally, the issue as to whether or not a new kind of man is being born today will be decided by this generation's sense of social solidarity and responsibility. To a much larger degree, the future existence of Christianity as a viable life option (as opposed to a "precious" hobby such as the collection of miniature paintings) depends upon the resurgence of the original leftism of the Christian message throughout the fragmented universal church. Christianity was originally leftist; let us make no mistake about that. It arose among the poor and dispossessed, the enslaved and the conquered; among women and foreigners to the cities where they lived. Jesus was no cautious builder, but a visionary oriented to the people of the land, who threw his life away in pursuit of the goal of bringing the humble and suffering to a vision of God as Father. When one is poor and from a subjugated group, as Jesus was, often he has to throw away his life as the price of making an impact on society. Martin Luther

King, Jr., and Malcolm X could understand that.

The leftward angle of vision that is the Christian world view is not limited to the experiment with community ownership of goods reported in Acts 4:32–37, so regularly declared a failure by conservatives. No, the leftism of Christ's teaching is basic, for it places its emphasis on man, especially on the poor and the mistreated man, on the sinner, the outcast, the stranger. The scene of Christ's whipping the pigeon salesman in the Temple should settle the question about his attitude toward the spirit of commercial enterprise. We must measure the genuine left-wing nature of Christianity by the teachings and actions of Jesus, not by the understandable human failures of the early Christian disciples (Acts, ch. 5).

The genuine spiritual basis of the impulse toward leftist political activity is empathy (a feeling of social solidarity with other people), most especially of empathy with those in distress, pain, suffering (physical and psychical) and poverty. If one does not know what this means, he might begin his education by reading *Let Us Now Praise Famous Men*, by James Agee and Walker Evans.[21] The sensitive, Christian, upper-class poet, James Agee, after studying the lives of three tenant families in Alabama, felt forced to give his book the famous call of Marx: workers of the world unite and fight. Yet Agee was no Marxist—he was a decent man with Christian feelings.

Feed the hungry, clothe the naked, heal the sick, care for the widow and the orphan, visit the prisoner: these are the basic commandments for the leftist and the Christian. They are the marks by which, Jesus proclaimed, God will recognize his own on Judgment

Day. When the repressed and disinherited of the earth come into power, they will use the same criteria.

The Need for a Radical Christianity for the Seventies

To reiterate the tenets of the social gospel and sound the call to social conscience seems very tame, and even uncalled for, in the 1970's. All about us are at least the skeletons, if not the bodies, of dozens of agencies, church, private, and governmental, designed to meet people's social needs. To proclaim a social gospel surely shows the age of the writer, or his lack of comprehension of "what's going on"—or does it? Precisely *because* social activity (like civil rights) has become the "in" thing, has become domesticated, the emotions behind it "declawed" and "defanged," we must call for a renewal of the human feelings that prompt such programs. We need a full-blown Christianity of the left, which not only *does,* but *knows* why it does what it does.

The dangerous opportunity that lies in the present American crisis of conscience symbolized in My Lai IV and the court-martial of Lieutenant Calley is precisely the chance *now* to stand up and teach the dignity of all humanity *in deeds*. Our "crisis" is the opening in America's psychic awareness that harsh event after harsh event has punched through the plasticity of the television culture. We are in a spiritual bind, a blind alley of the collective soul. Now, in this movement of extremity, the humane message of Jesus Christ may be able to make contact with the residual humanity in modern men.

We *must* break through with the radical call to become human ourselves and to treat all other men as human beings. In order to guide our people, the church must find itself again. In the words of Chief Old Lodge Skins in the recent film *Little Big Man,* "The White man (American) is crazy. He is crazy because he doesn't know where the center of the world is." The sense of a sacred space and a sacred time, of limits to what man can do to himself, to others, to animals, and to the earth, has evaporated from the modern consciousness. The bearers of the new mentality must grow up spiritually, in the Pauline sense (I Cor. 2:12 to 3:2), and point anew to the limits on manipulation of man and environment that are necessary if man is to be a "human being." The words, the thoughts, the slogans, the songs, the poems, the books, the exemplary personalities, are here; they can be recovered from man's history and discovered in the present. Now we must demonstrate how these essential elements of humanity can be applied to our historical condition. Until a radical version of the gospel, true to the past as well as faithful to the present, appears and is put to work, we can expect continued unhappiness on a mass scale. We can expect the growth of institutional and governmental oppression. We can expect the continued rise and growth of personalities so alienated that they will be pushed toward rebellion. We can expect a geometric increase in the experiments of men and women who cannot live their lives half human and half machine. We can expect an increase in the bizarre and the syncretic. That is the *best* we can expect. Unless the church recovers its ancient and original revolutionary zeal and becomes, as a church, what a few laymen, priests, nuns, and ministers have already become, we can expect our society to deteriorate even more. We can expect the year 2000 to be so dehumanized that the prophecies about *1984* will seem like pleasant fairy tales. We can look forward to a cowardly new world beyond the saddest imagination of an Orwell or a Huxley. We can bite the bitter bullet of the knowledge that the power to change this direction of society was put into our hands by the youth culture of the 1970's, and we were too faithless, too weak, to use it.

Man is, beyond all else, incomplete. Man is a project still under construction. He is able to make himself into a soldier bent on destruction or a medical doctor dedicated to healing. Man, too, can change the direction his project is taking. The soldier can become a priest, a helper of the poor. The medical man can become greedy and seek to serve only the well-to-do. Man does not *have* freedom. God, the Christian believes, created man *as* freedom. Man as free can turn his powers to destruction or construction. His essential tragedy is that in choosing to destroy himself, he destroys others *and the world*. Man's potential glory is that in choosing to heal, to build, and to conserve his own spirit, he will heal, build, and conserve all other creatures and the very earth itself. If there is one thread that runs true through all the new alternative life-styles and competing images of man today, it is precisely this insight: Man is the potential completion of God's creation or the instrument of God's ultimate frustration.

NOTES

Preface

1. Jack Newfield, *A Prophetic Minority* (The New American Library of World Literature, Inc., 1966), p. 32.
2. *Ibid.*

Chapter 1. The Shattering of the Traditional Images of Man

1. Harold H. Titus, *Living Issues in Philosophy*, 4th ed. (American Book Company, 1964), pp. 143–149.
2. Desmond Morris, *The Naked Ape* (McGraw-Hill Book Company, Inc., 1967).
3. Alexander Pope, *An Essay of Man*, ed. by Maynard Mack (Yale University Press, 1951).
4. Kenneth Keniston, *Young Radicals* (Harcourt, Brace and World, Inc., 1968). Also see Margaret Mead, *Culture and Commitment* (Doubleday & Company, Inc., 1970).
5. *Ibid.*
6. See Hiley H. Ward, *Prophet of the Black Nation* (The Pilgrim Press, 1969).
7. Kate Millet, *Sexual Politics* (Doubleday & Company, Inc., 1970).

8. John C. Cooper, *The New Mentality* (The Westminster Press, 1969).

9. See Chester McArthur Destler, *American Radicalism 1865–1901* (Quadrangle Books, Inc., 1966). Franklin Delano Roosevelt once said: "Remember, remember always that all of us, and you and I especially, are descended from immigrants and revolutionists." (Speech to the DAR, April 21, 1938.)

10. G. W. F. Hegel, *The Phenomenology of Mind*, tr. by J. B. Baillie (Humanities Press, Inc., 1964).

11. See Herbert Marcuse, *Eros and Civilization* (Beacon Press, Inc., 1966); *One Dimensional Man* (Beacon Press, Inc., 1964); and *Soviet Marxism* (Columbia University Press, 1958). Also see John Raser, "Herbert Marcuse, A Sketch," *Psychology Today*, Vol. 4, No. 9 (Feb., 1971), pp. 38 f.

12. See David Reuben, *Everything You Always Wanted to Know About Sex—But Were Afraid to Ask* (Bantam Books, Inc., 1971).

13. Philip Slater, *The Pursuit of Loneliness: American Culture at the Breaking Point* (Beacon Press, Inc., 1970), p. 55.

14. *Ibid.*

15. See C. P. Snow, *The Two Cultures: And a Second Look*, 2d ed. (Cambridge University Press, 1964).

Chapter 2. TRANSITIONS TO THE NEW MAN

1. *The Kentucky Kernel*, April 5, 1971, p. 1 (University of Kentucky).

2. John C. Cooper, *The Turn Right* (The Westminster Press, 1970).

3. A statement by Theresa A. Weber, freshman, Eastern Kentucky University, fall, 1970. This quotation and those from other college students are used with their full permission.

4. *Ibid.*
5. *Ibid.*
6. The identity of this source is kept confidential.
7. *Ibid.*
8. Deborah Munsey, senior, Eastern Ky. University.
9. *Ibid.*

Chapter 3. NEW LIFE-STYLES FOR THE SEVENTIES

1. *Webster's Seventh New Collegiate Dictionary* (G. & C. Merriam Company, 1970), pp. 736–737. See Tom Hayden, *Rebellion and Repression* (The World Publishing Company, 1969).
2. R. D. Laing, *The Politics of Experience* (Ballantine Books, Inc., 1969).
3. Joseph Sittler. Quotations from a news release of the Lutheran Commission on Press, Radio and Television, Lutheran Church in America, Feb., 1971.
4. *Tempo*, Vol. 3, No. 1, Nov., 1970 (National Council of Churches).
5. Eldridge Cleaver, *Soul on Ice* (McGraw-Hill Book Company, Inc., 1967).
6. *Ibid.*
7. *The Los Angeles Free Press* (Los Angeles, Calif.).
8. *The Great Speckled Bird* (Atlanta, Ga.).
9. *The Village Voice* (New York, N.Y.).
10. *The Blue-Tailed Fly* (Lexington, Ky.).
11. Cooper, *The New Mentality*.
12. *The Whole Earth Catalog*. Portola Institute.
13. See Marshall McLuhan and Quentin Fiore, *The Medium Is the Massage* (Bantam Books, Inc., 1967).
14. Cooper, *The Turn Right*.
15. Charles A. Reich, *The Greening of America* (Random House, Inc., 1970).
16. See "Persons of Interest," *Life,* Vol. 70, No. 11 (March 26, 1971), pp. 20–27.

166 A NEW KIND OF MAN

17. This material is freely adapted from information and letters furnished by Bruce Lee Cooper, of Mooresville, N.C.

18. *Ibid.*
19. *Ibid.*
20. *Ibid.*
21. *Ibid.*
22. *Ibid.*
23. *Ibid.*

Chapter 4. LIFE-STYLES—
THE INFORMED AND CONFORMED

1. A statement made by Theresa A. Weber, freshman, Eastern Kentucky University, fall, 1970.

2. *Ibid.*

3. Cooper, *The New Mentality.*

4. Charles A. Reich, *The Greening of America.*

5. Terry Rankin, philosophy major, Eastern Kentucky University, 1971.

6. Theresa A. Weber, *op. cit.*

7. *Jesus Christ Superstar.* Lyrics by Tim Rice, musical score by Andrew Lloyd Webber (Decca Records, A Division of MCA Inc., N.Y., 1970).

8. Theresa A. Weber, *op. cit.*

9. Rev. Edward Walline, Pastor, Emmanuel Evangelical Lutheran Church, 725 High Street, Racine, Wis. 53402. This essay was published in the Jan., 1971, issue of the parish paper, *The Evangel.*

10. Poem by John C. Cooper, used in Campus liturgy, Faith Lutheran Church, Lexington, Ky., Christmas, 1969 (for University of Kentucky students).

11. *Ibid.* Poem by John C. Cooper.

12. Brian Vachon, "The Jesus Movement Is Upon Us," *Look,* Vol. 35, No. 3 (Feb. 9, 1971).

13. Theresa A. Weber, *op. cit.*

14. Deborah Strong, Eastern Kentucky University, spring, 1971.

15. Reich, *op. cit.*

16. Cooper, *The New Mentality.*

17. Poem by John C. Cooper.

18. Information from Luis Marden, "Titicaca, Abode of the Sun," *National Geographic Magazine*, Vol. 139, No. 2 (Feb., 1971), pp. 272–294. The observations on the South American Indians made here bear out a thesis I formed in the summer of 1970 when my brother, my son, a student of mine, and I went on a walking tour of southern Mexico and talked with the farmers of the "backwoods."

19. Cooper, *The New Mentality.*

20. Reich, *op. cit.*

21. I think Reich's division of the old mentality (as I named it in 1969) into *two distinct sections* is tremendously helpful and I want to use this procedure here.

22. Rudolf Otto, *The Idea of the Holy* (Oxford University Press, Inc., 1936).

23. Philip Slater, *The Pursuit of Loneliness,* p. 15.

24. Fedor Dostoyevsky, *Crime and Punishment* (W. W. Norton & Company, Inc., 1964).

25. Albert Camus, *The Plague* (Modern Library, Inc., 1948).

Chapter 5. RELIGION IN AN AQUARIAN MODE

1. *Jesus Christ Superstar* (Decca Records, A Division of MCA Inc., N.Y., 1970).

2. "Jesus Freaks," the Student Senate colloquy at Eastern Kentucky University, Richmond, Ky., spring semester, 1971.

3. Pär Lagerkvist, *Barabbas* (Random House, Inc., 1951).

4. *Jesus Christ Superstar.*

5. Lawrence Ferlinghetti, *A Coney Island of the Mind* (New Directions, 1958).

6. I have many letters from radical Christian friends that say, in effect, "It is hard for a radical Christian to get—and keep—a job." This placing of one's career on the line is true in both church and academic circles. Nevertheless, many have crossed the line to a radical commitment and know (and no longer care) that there is no turning back.

7. Cooper, *The Turn Right*.

8. Most of the information included here on the Jesus Freaks was kindly provided to the author by James R. Blair, of Louisville, Ky., philosophy major, Eastern Kentucky University, spring, 1971.

9. Earl C. Gottschalk, Jr., " 'Jesus Freaks' Quit Revolution, Drugs for Fundamentalism; They Offend & Anger Some," *The Wall Street Journal*, March 2, 1971.

10. *Ibid.*

11. Arthur Blessitt, letter of March 3, 1971, to James R. Blair.

12. Brian Vachon, *loc. cit.*

13. Biblical tract, distributed by the "Children of God," Thurber, Tex.

14. James Dublin, "Thurber Commune Only High on Jesus," *The Abilene Reporter-News*, July 24, 1970.

15. Duane Pederson, editor, *Hollywood Free Paper*, letter of March 22, 1971.

16. James R. Blair, *loc. cit.*

Chapter 6. THE PRESENT REVOLUTION—
A DANGEROUS OPPORTUNITY

1. The quotation is from a statement given the author by Sandra Sommer, a philosophy major at Eastern Kentucky University, spring, 1970.

2. *Ibid.*

3. John C. Cooper, *The Roots of the Radical Theology* (The Westminster Press, 1967).

4. Cooper, *The New Mentality.*

5. Some of the more important books and resources, readily available, that will help the reader to understand the present social, political, educational, and spiritual situation, include:

Cooper, John C., *The New Mentality.* The Westminster Press, 1969.

Galbraith, John Kenneth, *The New Industrial State.* Houghton Mifflin Company, 1967.

Goodman, Mitchell, *A New America.* The Pilgrim Press, 1970.

Keniston, Kenneth, *Young Radicals.* Harcourt, Brace and World, Inc., 1968.

Kofsky, Frank, *Black Nationalism and the Revolution in Music.* Pathfinder Press, Inc., 1970.

Marcuse, Herbert, *Eros and Civilization.* Beacon Press, Inc., 1955.

—— *One Dimensional Man.* Beacon Press, Inc., 1964.

Reich, Charles A., *The Greening of America.* Random House, Inc., 1970.

Rolling Stone, March 4, 1971. (Newspaper). Straight Arrow Publishers, Inc.

Roszak, Theodore, *The Making of a Counter-Culture.* Doubleday & Company, Inc., 1969.

Theobald, Robert, *An Alternative Future for America II,* 2d ed. The Swallow Press, Inc., 1971.

Toffler, Alvin, *Future Shock.* Random House, Inc., 1970.

Whole Earth Catalog, The. Portola Institute.

6. Marshall McLuhan and Quentin Fiore, *War and Peace in the Global Village* (Bantam Books, Inc., 1968).

7. Paul Tillich, *Love, Power and Justice* (Oxford University Press, 1954); *Morality and Beyond* (Harper

& Row, Publishers, Inc., 1963). Reinhold Niebuhr, *Moral Man and Immoral Society* (Charles Scribner's Sons, 1932).

8. The following is a partial list of the many books on environmental problems that are available in any large bookstore:

Anderson, Walt (ed.), *Politics and Environment*. Goodyear Publishing Company, Inc., 1970.

Bates, Marston, *The Forest and the Sea*. A Vintage Book, Random House, Inc., 1960.

Bernarde, Melvin A., *Our Precarious Habitat*. W. W. Norton & Company, Inc., 1970.

Crisis of Survival, The, by the eds. of The Progressive and the College Div. of Scott, Foresman. William Morrow & Company, Inc., 1970.

Curtis, Richard, and Hogan, Elizabeth, *Perils of the Peaceful Atom*. Ballantine Books, Inc., 1969.

De Bell, Garrett (ed.), *The Environmental Handbook*. Ballantine Books, Inc., 1970.

Ehrlich, Paul R., *The Population Bomb*. Ballantine Books, Inc., 1970.

Godfrey, Arthur (ed.), *The Arthur Godfrey Environmental Reader*. Ballantine Books, Inc., 1970.

Hardin, Garrett (ed.), *Population, Evolution and Birth Control,* 2d ed. W. H. Freeman and Company, 1969.

Resources and Man, Committee on Resources and Man, National Academy of Sciences & National Research Council. W. H. Freeman and Company, 1969.

Swatek, Paul, *User's Guide to the Protection of the Environment*. Ballantine Books, Inc., 1969.

United Nations Report, *Chemical and Biological Weapons and the Effects of Their Possible Use*. Ballantine Books, Inc., 1970.

9. See "Protean Man," by Robert Jay Lifton, research psychiatrist at Yale, in Leo Hamalian and F. R. Karl (eds.), *The Radical Vision: Essays for the Seventies*

(Thomas Y. Crowell Company, 1970), pp. 43–58.

10. Cooper, *The New Mentality*, p. 27.

11. Don Mitchell, *Thumb Tripping* (Bantam Books, Inc., 1971).

12. See John C. Cooper, *Religion in the Age of Aquarius* (The Westminster Press, 1971).

13. This material was first presented by the author at a convocation at Pfeiffer College, Misenheimer, N.C., on March 12, 1971.

14. Frantz Fanon, tr. by Constance Farrington, *The Wretched of the Earth* (Grove Press, Inc., 1968).

15. As in the area around Kannapolis, N.C., and in many sections of North and South Carolina.

16. Jack Newfield, "The Death of Liberalism," *Playboy*, Vol. 18, No. 4 (April, 1971), p. 98.

17. *Ibid.*, p. 99.

18. *Ibid.*

19. Newfield, *A Prophetic Minority*.

20. Phyllis Schlafly, *A Choice Not an Echo* (Père Marquette Press, 1964).

21. James Agee and Walker Evans, *Let Us Now Praise Famous Men* (Ballantine Books, Inc., 1970).

143 - Rel. today

Ex p 36 - A child born today in United Kingdom stands 10 times greater chance of being admitted to a mental hospital than to a university; about $\frac{1}{5}$ of admissions are schizophrenic

p 59 - shift to inward emphasis among youth

p 86 - "You have to be smarter to be "poor" than to be "well off."